AW... WITH WORDS

Young Writers' 16th Annual Poetry Competition

It is feeling and force of imagination that make us eloquent.

How can I not dream while writing? The blank page gives a right to dream.

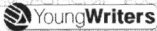

Poems From The Midlands
Edited by Heather Killingray

First published in Great Britain in 2007 by:
Young Writers
Remus House
Coltsfoot Drive
Peterborough
PE2 9JX
Telephone: 01733 890066
Website: www.youngwriters.co.uk

All Rights Reserved

© Copyright Contributors 2007

SB ISBN 978-1 84431 297 9

Foreword

This year, the Young Writers' *Away With Words* competition proudly presents a showcase of the best poetic talent selected from thousands of up-and-coming writers nationwide.

Young Writers was established in 1991 to promote the reading and writing of poetry within schools and to the young of today. Our books nurture and inspire confidence in the ability of young writers and provide a snapshot of poems written in schools and at home by budding poets of the future.

The thought, effort, imagination and hard work put into each poem impressed us all and the task of selecting poems was a difficult but nevertheless enjoyable experience.

We hope you are as pleased as we are with the final selection and that you and your family continue to be entertained with *Away With Words Poems From The Midlands* for many years to come.

Contents

Laynah Nathan (12)   1

Castle Vale School & Specialist Performing Arts College, Castle Vale

Emily Gordon (12)   2
Samantha Bowkett (12)   3
Alice Selby (11)   4
Aleah Hobbs (11)   5
Stella Dymock-Courts (12)   6
Chloe Arnold (12)   7
Julia Franks (12)   8
Rosie Harding (11)   9

Great Wyrley Performing Arts High School, Walsall

Rebecca Smallman (13)   10
Luke Plimmer (13)   11
Ben Smallman & Grant Tonks (13)   12
Jacob Stokes & Josh Pearce (12)   13
Callum Smith & Chris Turner (12)   14
Sam Layland (11)   15
Lauren Allman (12)   16
Lucy Hale (11)   17
Tom Lycett (12)   18
Matt Lockley (12)   19
Megan King (12)   20
Abi Yarnold (12)   21
Natalie Jones (12)   22
Bethany Lewis (12)   23
Jessica Jones (12)   24
Natalie Murray (11)   25
Danielle Haden (12)   26
Jake Tinkler (11)   27
Sophie Stokes (12)   28
Meredith Allen (12)   29

Joseph Leckie Community College, Walsall

Spencer Smith (12)   30
Rizwanah Sallu (11)   31

Amer Yasim	32
Moqeet Tariq (11)	33
Haris Javed (12)	34
Haashim Data (12)	35
Amie Smith (12)	36
Rachael Sarah Plant (11)	37
Deena Begum (12)	38
Alexandra Cliff (12)	39
Gurpreet Kaur Sohal (12)	40
Sarah Arshad (12)	41
Hasina Begum (12)	42

Lyng Hall School, Coventry

Shayla Bowen (11)	43
Lisa Duffin (12)	44
Kyra Bhuee (12)	45
Elizabeth Heath (12)	46
Rebecca Hambridge (12)	47

Pedmore Technology College, Pedmore

Jake Newey (12)	48
Thomas Clift (12)	49
Madelaine Simon (11)	50
Josh Cartwright (13)	51
Becci Irwin (12)	52
Daniel Gilliam (13)	53
Andrew Forrest (13)	54
James Didehvar (12)	55
Becky Hughes (13)	56
Adiba Mahmood (13)	57
Bethany Hale (12)	58
Jodie Bostock (12)	59
Suhail Ali (12)	60
Sophie Radford (13)	62
Ryan McCullagh (11)	63
Molly Harper (11)	64
Alexandra Steventon (12)	66
Matthew Knowles (12)	67
Kirsty Parker (12)	68
Ali Hussain (12)	69
Luke Jefferies (12)	70

Kerri Louise Garbett (13)	71
Tammy Cox (13)	72
Anjeela Wakeel (13)	73
Chelsea Savoy (11)	74
Chloe McMurray (12)	75
Lydia Campbell (12)	76
Eloise Mount (13)	77
Liam Taylor (12)	78
Adam Hodges (12)	79
Amy Timmins (12)	80
Zarcur Dard (12)	81
Mary Senier (12)	82
Aneisha Jones (12)	83
Gabby Harris (12)	84
Joanne Kay (11)	85
Ellis Hodnette (12)	86
Sammie Pardoe (12)	87
Laura Banks (12)	88
Alice Nicholls (12)	89
Philip Huxley (12)	90
Harry Till (11)	91
Jack Deeley (12)	92

Perryfields High School

Ashleigh Simpson (14)	93
Shalayna Hutchinson (16)	94

Pool Hayes Arts & Community School, Willenhall

Zach Howells (12)	95
Sarah Joynes (12)	96
Ashley Jones (12)	97
Morganna Lewis (12)	98
Nicole Thiara (12)	100
Alana Klyvis (11)	101

Shireland Colligate Academy, Smethwick

Sasha Stanley-Gaussen (12)	102
Nemeesha Patel (11)	103
Grace Meah	104
Rameez Akhtar	105

Eleanor Cann (12)	106
Minerva Pawsey (12)	108
Sarasuati Jaiswal	109
Gratitude Katega (11)	110
Jagvir Garcha (12)	111
Harjit Jandu (12)	112

Sutton Coldfield Grammar School for Girls, Sutton Coldfield

Anisah Mahatay (11)	113
Saba Asam (12)	114
Caroline Jeffery (12)	115
Heather Jenkins (12)	116
Regan Barry (12)	117
Eleanor Knight (12)	118
Jennifer Cooper (12)	119
Imogen Marriott (12)	120
Kerry Bird (11)	121
Marissa Xam (12)	122
Jamilah Campbell (13)	123
Palma Kashyap (13)	124
Anna Owen (13)	125
Chloe Thompson-Haynes (13)	126
Laurel Windsor (13)	127
Ajit Kaur Sagoo (13)	128
Niharika Chadha (13)	130
Frances Hancock (13)	131
Areeba Tahir (12)	132
Natasha Branson (12)	133
Rebecca Sheehan (12)	134
Moyo Bajomo (12)	135
Haleema Mahmood (12)	136
Victoria Stephenson (12)	137
Katey MacAllister (12)	138
Isobel Wilkinson (12)	139
Claire Guest (12)	140
Satkartar Chandan (11)	141
Laura Sumner (13)	142

The City Technology College, Kingshurst

Rachel Hawkins (12)	143
Kimari Strachan (12)	144

Kieran Reilly (12)	145
Lewis Jones (11)	146
Niall Coney	147
James Dowling	148
Samuel Bibb (12)	149
Alexander Brock (11)	150
Liam Hehir (12)	151
Chelsea Jones (12)	152
Siana-Rose Crawford (12)	153
Shannon Kavanagh (12)	154
Hollie Rodgers (11)	155
Tahlia Banks (12)	156
Eleanor Lane (12)	157
Jadene Weldon (12)	158
Alexandra Daykin (11)	159
Louis Herbert (12)	160
Jack Grant (12)	161
Lauren Sadler (11)	162
Kieran Gould (11)	163
Thomas Murphy (11)	164
Harry Charles (12)	165
Kayleigh Bricknell (12)	166
Andrew Morris (12)	167
Mikey Jarvis (12)	168
Lindsey Peach (12)	169
Amy Robinson (12)	170
Daishia Holmes (12)	171

Tividale Community Arts College, Tividale

Tisa Carroll (12)	172
Christopher Bagley (12)	173
Emma Swift (12)	174
Kirsty Pilsbury (12)	175
Atang Ncube (12)	176
Joe Harris (12)	177
Manraj Dhinsa (12)	178
Nicola Weaver (11)	179

Tudor Grange School, Solihull

Rhianna Centurion-Eyre (11)	180
Amelia Ebdon (15)	181

David Todd (15)	182
James Henrick (11)	183
Felicity Zakers (12)	184
Surbhi Kenth (14) & Emma Quirk (15)	185
Emily Dean (13)	186
Sophia Harley (13)	187
Hans Ramzan (12)	188
Fiona Pearce (13)	189

The Poems

Do We Think?

Do we think about the days when it's rainy and cold?
Do we think about people with just a shelter, but no home?
Do we think about all the dangers in the world?
Do we think about the teenage pregnant girls?
Do we think about the people who are too scared to go outside?
Do we think about the people who commit suicide?
Do we think about the people who are always sad?
Do we think about the children who get abused by their
                                      mums and dads?
Do we think about what would happen if we all weren't friends?
If we did, we would soon realise that this world
Would have a quick end.

Laynah Nathan (12)

Alone

I look up at the stars
And see a lonely
Place of darkness.

A planet filled with
Darkness, light, sorrow
And joy.

An adventure awaits
You every time you step out
Of your door.

You never know what tomorrow
Might bring, happiness or sadness
A light at the end of your tunnel.

We walk upon mystery each day
A place of history and life.

Whether people are evil or show
Kindness and open their doors
Our mind and feelings make us human
And nothing more.

That fights for survival each day
Among millions of minds and bodies
Whether rich or poor we fight together
And we beat as one alone in the darkness
Among the stars.

Emily Gordon (12)
Castle Vale School & Specialist Performing Arts College, Castle Vale

Lost

You wander in the fields of gold,
Where you will find your true love's soul.
If you find it, you are at rest,
If you don't, you will have stress.

As you quietly walk around,
You will see what you have found,
When you see your surprise,
You will see it at sunrise.

Sunrise is your only clue,
If you find that it is true,
If you happen to see a deer,
Make sure that it has no fear.

As you come near the deer,
You will see something clear,
When you find it, it's your gold,
Then you've found your true love's soul.

Samantha Bowkett (12)
Castle Vale School & Specialist Performing Arts College, Castle Vale

Valentine's Poem

Your smile spreads across the Earth,
Bringing happiness at every birth.
Your sadness creeps, but is never heard,
As happiness defeats it.

Your cheeks are brighter than the sun,
Even if there is no fun.
Your sadness has not yet won,
As happiness defeats it.

Your lips are cherries, they glow so bright,
As the sun shows its light.
Your sadness has lost the fight,
As happiness defeats it.

Your heart has left a mark on mine,
I love it as it drinks and dines.
Your sadness cannot combine,
As happiness defeats it.

Alice Selby (11)
Castle Vale School & Specialist Performing Arts College, Castle Vale

The Space Poem

Right up there, where the stars are bright,
I'd stay right away, they will blind you with their light.

Asteroids and planets, all floating around,
Somewhere out there, where there is no sound.

Out there, in the distance, a wide open space,
Bright lights and great colours, what a wonderful place!

The golden sun, with its deadly beam,
Its big, round shape, its special gleam.

The exciting galaxies and the weird Milky Way,
Scary, starry darkness, even during the day.

Out there, where the Earth is far, far out,
Space is what this poem is all about.

Aleah Hobbs (11)
Castle Vale School & Specialist Performing Arts College, Castle Vale

The Spider

First he's in the bathroom
Then he's in the hall
Then he's in the kitchen
I can't stand it at all!

Then he's in my bedroom
I nearly had a fright
Then he crawled all over me
In the middle of the night!

Stella Dymock-Courts (12)
Castle Vale School & Specialist Performing Arts College, Castle Vale

Stop The Pain!

I can't take the pain any longer,
They'd be better off without me,
I just want it all to stop,
I have become a punchbag.

The girls didn't realise it
They were becoming murderers,
Nor did my friends and family
Think something was wrong,
My body has become weak now,
I shove the pills in my mouth.

I wake to find my mum crying,
I try to tell her I'm OK,
She just won't stop sobbing,
Then it all goes dark.

I'm dead,
What have I done?
My pain has stopped now
And it will never come back,
But for my friends and family,
The pain is only just beginning!

Chloe Arnold (12)
Castle Vale School & Specialist Performing Arts College, Castle Vale

My Eyes

Look into my eyes, what do you see?
I see upset children whirling around me.
They're hungry and ill, with nowhere to live,
Some are very skinny and some can't see,
They're just upset children, whirling around me.

Look into my eyes, what do you see?
I see old, sick people crying for me,
They are nearly dying because they need help,
I wish I was there to care, but I know I can't be there.

Julia Franks (12)
Castle Vale School & Specialist Performing Arts College, Castle Vale

Look Into My Eyes

Look into my eyes, what do you see?
I see a roller coaster waiting for me,
I run up the stairs,
Wait in the line,
All my friends are saying,
'It's OK, you will be fine.'
I sit in my seat,
All I can feel is my heart go *beat, beat,*
Finally, it decides to start,
I don't feel safe, because I am at the end of the cart.

Look into my eyes, what do you see?
I'm frightened and scared,
Someone, please help me,
My hands clenched onto my seat,
My heart beating faster
And my eyes at my feet,
It's going upside down,
It still needs to go round and round,
The ride is done,
In the end, it turned out to be a load of fun!

Rosie Harding (11)
Castle Vale School & Specialist Performing Arts College, Castle Vale

The Dungeon In France

I sat in a dark corner and groaned,
There, opposite me, was a bag of bones.
The bones got up and jiggled and danced,
This was no ordinary dungeon in France.

There were bats barking like dogs,
There were spiders with prickles like hedgehogs.
The handcuffs got down and pranced,
This was no ordinary dungeon in France.

There were cats with feathers,
There were dogs made of leather.
There were birds in advance,
This was no ordinary dungeon in France.

There were worms with hair,
In that dark, gloomy lair.
There was a sandman called Lance,
Never go to the dungeon in France!

Rebecca Smallman (13)
Great Wyrley Performing Arts High School, Walsall

Déjà Vu

You sleep at night and dream about tomorrow
You wake up in the morning and your dream comes true
Déjà vu is a freaky thing
But if you have a good dream
It could be an amazing thing
Try to dream about the future
It might come true
It might just haunt you
But if it is real déjà vu
It is what you dreamed all night through.

Luke Plimmer (13)
Great Wyrley Performing Arts High School, Walsall

Hanging Around

The wire is sharp and also thin
Just like a needle or a pin
Revenge grows bigger and hearts get weak
Food and water is what they seek.

Helpless hands and crumbling bones
Cries of suffering and desperate moans
They look so strong, but inside they're not
Their dirty clothes are all they've got.

The burning heat can change a man
They might have been captured by the Taliban
A cup of water, a crumb of bread
With this a day, they could be dead.

Distressed and dirty and lonesome inside
By these rules they must abide
Rule one, to them is keeping quiet
With the food they get, it's like a diet.

Rules to us are really easy
When we drink water, it's like we're royalty
They keep their heads down
Without a whisper, without a frown.

Ben Smallman & Grant Tonks (13)
Great Wyrley Performing Arts High School, Walsall

Hallowe'en

It's the 31st
You know what that means,
Time for frights
Shouts and screams.

I like to dress
As the Grim Reaper,
Everyone says
'Jeepers creepers!'

Knock on the door
Or ring the bell,
'Trick or treat'
The monsters yell.

The pumpkin is
A scary sight,
With fiery eyes
Staring into the night.

Hallowe'en is what
I like the most,
Dress up to scare
And to boast.

We've got our bags
And spooky disguises,
Time to go
And collect our prizes.

We eat up all
Of our tasty sweets,
Lollipops and
Chocolate treats.

If you think
You shook with fear,
Just you wait
Until next year!

Jacob Stokes & Josh Pearce (12)
Great Wyrley Performing Arts High School, Walsall

The Stunner

S tone cold stunner
T hink son
O h no
N ever do it again
E ver again

C an of whoops
O h damn
L ay the Smackdown
D on't drop my bear!

Callum Smith & Chris Turner (12)
Great Wyrley Performing Arts High School, Walsall

What Am I?

My first is in sauce and also in pistachios
My second is in prawn but not in cheese
My third is in sausages and also in squid
My fourth is in chicken but not in turkey
My fifth is in sandwiches and is in cottage pie
My sixth is in potatoes but not in carrots
My seventh is in pineapple and in mango
My last is in naan bread but not in rice.

What am I?

I am a . . . ?

Sam Layland (11)
Great Wyrley Performing Arts High School, Walsall

Jealousy

I want what she's got,
She's everything I'm not.

I want to be cool,
But I'm taken for a fool.

I try to fit in,
I just can't win.

I've done everything to make her keen,
All she does, is be mean.

I've got the latest game,
But she still thinks I'm really lame.

She's taken all my friends,
The torture never ends.

Lauren Allman (12)
Great Wyrley Performing Arts High School, Walsall

Dog Kennings

Loud barker
Ball fetcher
Stick chaser
Wet noser
Face licker
Fast runner
Quick panter
Good hearer
Great smeller
Hole digger
Bone burier.

D ig holes to bury bones in
O wn toys and love to play
G ood at smelling and hearing
S mell food from far away.

Lucy Hale (11)
Great Wyrley Performing Arts High School, Walsall

The Match

Match/extra time

Once you start, you can't stop
One, two, maybe three
If your winger is Liz-Tee

Round and leather
It's not fine weather
You smell wet grass
They make a pass

Shouting, cheering
Your face gleaming
Go on, you're there
Silence, despair

On your head
Ouch! You may want your bed
There is a gleam
You saved your team

Penalties

Oh no, you're 5-4 down
You can't help but frown
What a save, you're back in this
Oh, what a miss!

You win, you win
Shouts Lynn
You're shocked to the bone
But one thing's for certain
You'll never walk alone.

Tom Lycett (12)
Great Wyrley Performing Arts High School, Walsall

Monkey Kennings

Tree swinger
Lice eater
Banana muncher
Leaf nibbler
Loud chatterer
Gold coloured
Tail twirling
Monkey.

Matt Lockley (12)
Great Wyrley Performing Arts High School, Walsall

The Dolphin

She hides below the deep lagoon,
She glides amongst the tides,
Upon the passing waves she rides,
As the sunset slowly sets.

Megan King (12)
Great Wyrley Performing Arts High School, Walsall

Summer Holidays

S uper days
U nder the sun
M agnificent holidays
M essing about on the beach
E ating ice creams
R oaring waves

H awking seagulls
O nly a few days left
L et's make the most of it
I t has been great so far
D own on the beach for the last time
A nnoying, annoying, too soon to go
Y es, we will be back
S o sad leaving though.

Abi Yarnold (12)
Great Wyrley Performing Arts High School, Walsall

Holidays!

H aving fun
O n holiday
L ying back
I n the sun
D ancing forever
A ll just for fun
Y ou wouldn't want to miss this
S uper fun for everyone.

Natalie Jones (12)
Great Wyrley Performing Arts High School, Walsall

Rabbit Kennings

Plant eater
Long sleeper
Floppy ears
High jumper
Thick fur.

Bethany Lewis (12)
Great Wyrley Performing Arts High School, Walsall

Snowflakes

S now falls upon the ground
N ice hot cups of hot chocolate
O n some nights carol singers sing
W inter is here!
F rost fills the air
L et's have a snowball fight
A ll my decorations are on my tree
K ick some snowflakes off a branch
E veryone is wrapped up warm
S now people fill this country's floor!

Jessica Jones (12)
Great Wyrley Performing Arts High School, Walsall

The Sweet Shop

Sweets up there,
Sweets everywhere!
Look! There's my favourite choice
A huge jar of white mice!

Children cry,
Over what sweet to buy.
A jelly worm
That could even squirm!

Little rings,
Are quite delicate things,
Letters are hard,
They taste like card!

Rhubarb and custard,
Is better than mustard,
A cough sweet
Not worth the treat.

Maybe a toffee
Is better than coffee,
So what is your favourite sweet?
And remember, is it worth the treat?

Natalie Murray (11)
Great Wyrley Performing Arts High School, Walsall

N.Murray

Grandad,
Here is my poem, hope you like it.
Nats!!!

The Slimy Slurk
(Based on 'The Slither Slurk')

Down beneath the frog swamp,
Down beneath the reeds,
Down beneath the fishpond,
Down beneath the weeds.
Among the sludgy ditches,
Among the misty murk,
Beneath the gloomy shadows,
Lives the silver, slimy slurk.

Lives the silver slurk
And the silver slurk's a thing,
Makes a sound of whistling
And a clammy kind of *cling*.
Warts along its shoulders,
Spikes coming off its nose,
Big, bright yellow teeth and tongue,
No nails on its toes.

The slurk is known for stalking,
Creeps when you are walking.

Don't ever trust the slimy slurk,
You won't come back alive!

Danielle Haden (12)
Great Wyrley Performing Arts High School, Walsall

What Am I?

I am made from cows' milk
I sometimes have hazelnut in
I can be orange flavoured
I am creamy.
You open your eyes to a surprise
I lie in the fridge for a special occasion
I can have air bubbles in me
There are lots of people who eat me
You enjoy me at any time of the day.

What am I?

Answer: chocolate.

Jake Tinkler (11)
Great Wyrley Performing Arts High School, Walsall

The Dog Kennings

Leg biter
Toy chewer
Cat chaser
Fuss maker
Shoe taker
Bone burier.

Sophie Stokes (12)
Great Wyrley Performing Arts High School, Walsall

Football Kennings

Feet smashing
Crowd lashing
Goal scoring
Coach yawning
Ball bouncing
Keeper pouningr
Fans cheering
Allies fearing.

A: a football match.

Meredith Allen (12)
Great Wyrley Performing Arts High School, Walsall

The Bullies

I go to school, scared every day,
Of bullies who take my money away.
I walk to school alone every day,
That's the start of my normal school day.

I get kicked and pushed up the wall,
By people who are big and tall.
They take my pens and pencils too,
They even throw them down the loo.

I feel lonely in every way,
The bullies took my money away.
I walk home alone every day,
That's a poem of my normal school day.

Spencer Smith (12)
Joseph Leckie Community College, Walsall

The Blue Dragon

The sea is a flaming dragon,
Enormous and blue,
He stomps on the beach all day,
With his sharp teeth eating the fish all day.

With his wings pushing the waves against cliffs,
Roaring at the dull, dark days,
Then comes the sun
And he sits in the sea so quietly
And goes to sleep.

Rizwanah Sallu (11)
Joseph Leckie Community College, Walsall

Bullying

Stop abusing me!
You're putting me down!
Don't shout at me!
No hitting me!
Stop playing mind games with me!
Don't boss me around!
Stop hurting me!
Stop telling me where I can or cannot go!
Stop sending me threatening messages!

Stop bullying!

Amer Yasin
Joseph Leckie Community College, Walsall

The Sea

This sea is a roaring lion
Yellow and orange
He roars on the beach ever day
He uses his sharp teeth and scary eyes
He scares everyone every day
He also eats human beings.

Moqeet Tariq (11)
Joseph Leckie Community College, Walsall

Street Life Of London!

The street life
Kids in the street, carrying a knife
People killing each other, thinking it's funny
People would do anything around here
For money

Nobody has feelings in the hood
People round the corner selling Bud

Everyone here has got their own ground
If someone kills you
They will be crowned the London King
There has ever been found.

Haris Javed (12)
Joseph Leckie Community College, Walsall

Bullying

Monday morning I walked through the corridors,
When they pinched my books and threw them around,
I picked them up, they kept nudging me.
Bruised all over,
What clever children!
There was no one there,
To witness their nastiness.
The teacher came; they blamed it on me,
I know I didn't do it,
But what will happen to me?
I'm so unhappy,
My mum thinks I'm ill,
I don't even want to go to school.
My friends say, 'Report them!'
Otherwise things will stay the same,
I tell my favourite teacher, who says,
'I will stop their game.'
I feel better now,
The boys have left, I know I was a fool,
To stay quiet all along.
I'm no longer afraid,
To go to lessons
And I'm glad it's all over.

Haashim Data (12)
Joseph Leckie Community College, Walsall

Those Boys

I was sitting by an old oak tree,
When a bee came and stung me,
Then I heard these boys,
With their huge sticks,
Coming to get me.

I got up and ran as fast as I could,
Then I tripped and the boys got me,
They took my glasses and stamped on them
And I could not see,
All I saw was arms and hands
Grabbing me tight up a tree.

Then they went and I was lonely and hurt,
I wanted to be at home with my family
And to make some friends.

Amie Smith (12)
Joseph Leckie Community College, Walsall

Homeless

Why am I homeless?
What did I do to deserve this?
I sit in the streets watching the children make fun of me,
I have no money to buy any food for me.
I go around and ask for money,
But people just go, *'Shoo! Shoo!'*
I go in a corner and have a little cry,
Then go back in the streets to find some food for me.
I don't know who my mum is,
I want to find her though.
My dad died a couple of years ago,
Then my evil stepmother chucked me out of the house.
So now I have to face up to the people who make fun of me
Because I am on the streets,
Why do people pick on me because I am on the streets?

Rachael Sarah Plant (11)
Joseph Leckie Community College, Walsall

Lonely And Fearful Girl

My friends told me to keep away,
From people with low intelligence,
Who wore dirty shoes and ragged clothes,
People that ran in the hills
And bathed in muddy water.

On my own again,
Walking slowly home,
I heard noises like jaguars
Ready to attack.

I was shivering with fear,
They grabbed me hard, smothering me with mud,
I had tears in my eyes,
I felt like an ant ready to be trod on,
I wanted to scream and push them away.

But I could not bring myself to do it,
I was actually very ashamed,
While I had worn fine clothes,
They had ripped, torn clothes,
I felt pity for them and wanted to be friends,
But sadly, I didn't feel they wanted to.

Deena Begum (12)
Joseph Leckie Community College, Walsall

Meaning Of Life

What is the meaning of life?
It's only something we do the same every day,
It's going to end quickly,
It's too short and too lonely,
If only that great man in Heaven
Could help me stay alive for much more,
Look at the homeless and needy,
They won't be here for much longer,
I have no family and no friends
And no one to love me, no one to talk to.

No one would care if I just faded away
And my ashes would get mixed up
With some old newspaper,
I used to be rich and famous,
But all that disappeared over some stupid song,
I'm going to go now;
I will see you in Heaven . . .
Bye!

Alexandra Cliff (12)
Joseph Leckie Community College, Walsall

What Is Life All About?

What is the meaning of life?
We can be lonely or crowded,
At times we are happy,
But at others, very sad.

Why do we have family and friends?
Are they here to take care of us
And keep us happy?
Or are they here to earn money for us?

Did we come into the world
To wander and explore?

Are we always meant to be working hard?
Or are we allowed to be lazy at times?
For some, it is always!

Places are to see,
Or are we sent there for discovery?
What is the meaning of life?

Gurpreet Kaur Sohal (12)
Joseph Leckie Community College, Walsall

Bullying

I woke up in the middle of the night,
To dream about this fearful sight,
I shut my eyes and closed them tight,
But the dream would not go from my sight.

The terrifying bully was so near,
Filling me with lots of fear,
Oh! How I longed for my mum,
The bully made my fingers numb.

The bullies took my money away,
This is the story of a typical school day,
Now I go to lunch and see,
The bullies running after me.

Sarah Arshad (12)
Joseph Leckie Community College, Walsall

The Sea

The sea is an aggressive cat,
Giant and black,
He prowls on the beach all day,
Scratching against the rocks,
Hour upon hour he miaows,
The big heavy stones,
They fall, fall, fall, fall!

But on quiet days in June or July,
He sits there on the sandy shores,
So calm and quiet,
Watching the summer days go by.

Hasina Begum (12)
Joseph Leckie Community College, Walsall

My Poem

Shayla is my name,
I come from outer space,
The Sims 2 is my favourite game,
I walk at a fast pace,
My mates are in sets two, three, one,
My favourite teacher is Miss Bird,
I always make myself heard!

Shayla Bowen (11)
Lyng Hall School, Coventry

Dear Nan!

You were my north,
You were my south,
My east and west.

The love was hot,
But now it's cold,
It's like a part of me was sold.

No one was there,
Set for you and your hair,
When you died,
I wanted to hide,
Between us we had love
And your favourite bird was a dove.

We always had each other,
Doesn't matter where we are,
Even if we had a scare,
We always had each other.

Lisa Duffin (12)
Lyng Hall School, Coventry

The Newborn Bud

The newborn bud
Waiting for the raindrops
To sprinkle down
In a shower of bliss

The newborn bud
Waiting for a glow
To shine down
And guide it in the dark

The newborn bud
Waiting for the day
Where it finally blooms
Into the flower it is.

Kyra Bhuee (12)
Lyng Hall School, Coventry

Autumn

Twirling,
To the sound of the breeze,
The leaves are colourful,
All falling off trees,
Red, yellow, orange and green.

Autumn has lots of colourful moments,
The most colourful season of all,
When the trees are tall
And the leaves will fall,
That's what we call autumn.

Elizabeth Heath (12)
Lyng Hall School, Coventry

A Thing

There's a thing in my pocket that I can't explain,
It's sort o grey and sends my worries away,
Everyone wants to see it, but I say no, so . . .
If I showed you what was in my pocket,
Would you tell or keep quiet?
There's a thing in my pocket that I can't explain.

Rebecca Hambridge (12)
Lyng Hall School, Coventry

Night Lights

People running riot,
Guns shooting,
I was there.
Standing there, I was blind,
Blind as a bat,
But I had good hearing, thank God!
But I was dreaming, thank God!
I was in my bedroom
And for the first time in my life I could see
And the first thing I saw, was a bee,
I went to see the ocean,
My friends' football matches,
I went to see everything,
I could see again!
But I was a pain!

Jake Newey (12)
Pedmore Technology College, Pedmore

Night Light

It started in the night
As a tiny light
The light came towards me
It shone like a key
More and more lights appeared
Then stars disappeared
The lights stuck together to form a white light
At this point, it was giving me a fright,
Then the stars reappeared
And the lights disappeared
Then my mom shouted at me
'Turn off that TV!'

Thomas Clift (12)
Pedmore Technology College, Pedmore

Memories

A drippy ice cream,
The ooze that runs down my sleeve,
The stuff that makes my fingers sticky
And I wipe them on my mother's seam,
These were my memories!

My first day at primary school,
I was a mouse being chased by a lion, with fright,
That moves so softly through the night,
My heart, a drum, my legs like toothpicks,
These were my memories!

Trying to make a change at college,
To stop the testing of lots of poor pets,
I asked my friends to help,
They said it was for girls,
But I disagreed,
These were my memories!

Now I am old and crooked,
I suffer well,
My heart has stopped,
I needed air,
Those were all my memories!

Madelaine Simon (11)
Pedmore Technology College, Pedmore

Backwards And Beyond

Through my life I've come to realise, we're only stepping back,
Only peeking through the crack,
Of a future that could have been ours.
Wasting valuable hours,
Jumping and dancing with bells and flowers.
Our future comes at a toss of coin,
For whether we win, lose of suffer a loss.
Working away from sun up to sun down,
Cracking a smile or struggling a frown.
Thoughts of death and ill health appear,
As you sit there, drinking your beer.
Alone in the takeaway as you usually are,
Alone again, driving the car.
Closing windows and locking doors,
As I've said, we're always moving backwards.

Josh Cartwright (13)
Pedmore Technology College, Pedmore

Darkness Above

Darkness lies above
In the cold, shadowed night
My head, thumping with fear
And throbbing from the endless fall
I stagger back and you follow
You get closer, yet again
You strike out and the bloody stick hits my leg
I collapse and hit the ground
My memory goes blank . . .

I wake, lying in a dark alley
My heart racing with terror that you might come back
I stagger backwards, hopelessly
Reality hits me, where am I?
How long have I been here? Was it all a dream?
Just an end to a drunken night
Or a cruel and violent attack?

Then I realised who you really were
The person who I trusted most of all
They will never believe it
The goody-two-shoes, the know-it-all
He is the one that brought me pain
My brother.

Becci Irwin (12)
Pedmore Technology College, Pedmore

Should I?

Walking down the street,
Should I?
Turning down the alley,
Will I?
Entering the gun shop,
Can I?

Walking back down the street,
Reminiscing,
On the floor in my own blood,
Shadow over me,
Taunting me.

Knocking on the door,
The moment caught me,
I heard him say,
'I killed you,'
Then I heard a bang.
On the floor in blood,
My heart pounding,
Darkness taking me,
Famous last words,
I'm sorry my old friend.

I should have
Walked to the light,
I would have,
Nearly there,
I could have.

Daniel Gilliam (13)
Pedmore Technology College, Pedmore

The Robbery At Night

It was a dark and dreary night,
I waited quietly for something,
Anything to happen.

The clock struck twelve
And then it happened,
Out of the blue,
There was an explosion.

A big mix of red,
Yellow and orange,
Then a roar of cars.

They raced towards us,
In their vans, beeping
The horns madly.

We took aim,
With our guns,
At the wheels
And fired.

It happened so soon,
The tyres exploded
And the car
Was propelled,
Thirty feet into the air.

We walked over,
To the wreckage,
On the floor
And took the stolen goods.

We then walked away,
From the little, burning fire,
Caused by the burnt car.

We smiled and drove away
Leaving the mess
Of a robbery
Behind.

Andrew Forrest (13)
Pedmore Technology College, Pedmore

Crime, I Can't Stop

Crime . . . why do I do it?
The question unknown
The answer not told
As I wonder when I do it . . .
Nothing seems to happen

It's the same old steal
House by house
Road by road
Everything stole
When will they find out?

Crime . . .
I don't know why I do it
Crime . . .
Destroying you from the inside
Crime . . .
I am forced to do it
Crime . . .

Who it is
They do not know
As long as it's secret
Everything is unknown
That's the way it works . . .

Going through an open window
Which they accidentally left open
Stealing items
Or personal things
Will they ever know?

Crime . . .
I don't know why I do it
Crime . . .

Destroying you from the inside
Crime . . .
I am forced to do it
Crime . . .

James Didehvar (12)
Pedmore Technology College, Pedmore

Alone

Alone, afraid, your face darkened by the shadow of night,
The blade in your hand, concealed by the darkness.
I step away, you step closer,
Alone, afraid, I see your face.

Alone, afraid, you hit my pride,
My dignity smeared across the alley floor.
The betrayer steps up, acting the master,
Alone, afraid, I see your face.

Alone, afraid, my mind, it wanders,
Your endless memory, engraved in my thoughts.
Questions unanswered from times before,
Alone, afraid, I see you face.

Alone, afraid, you uncover your head,
What lies beneath, the face of death.
Your decision, betrayal,
Alone, afraid, I see your face.

Alone, afraid, you do the deed,
You run, I stay for one last breath.
Pain sears through my side for one last time,
Alone, afraid, my friend, my killer.

Becky Hughes (13)
Pedmore Technology College, Pedmore

So! I'm Black!

Sitting on the streets,
With nothing to eat,
People walk by,
All they give is a sigh,
Dirty looks because I have no books!

So, I'm black, what's the deal with that?
First class no,
Second class go!

Sitting down,
With a frown, I soon get kicked,
Now I'm getting really kicked,
I get up,
He looks and smacks me with his books,
I kick, he kicks,
Soon the police come to know
What I did, I feel so low!
Attacked and smacked,
I can't take it anymore;
I'm going to knock out this bloody door!
So, I'm in jail, with no one to bail!

All because I'm black!
What's the deal with that?

Adiba Mahmood (13)
Pedmore Technology College, Pedmore

As A Baby

I must be some kind of toy,
A fusspot that can only bring joy,
But when I cry, they cannot see,
That something is very wrong with me.

I want a pet, a dog maybe,
It is love that would make me see,
That everyone can be so kind,
Even animals that have no mind.

What about my mom and dad?
They never want me to feel so bad,
I seem to be the fattest thing,
But true happiness is what I bring.

Life is good, life gets sad,
But however it's you who should be glad,
Loads of money, not too rich,
It's better than being left in that ditch.

I'm so proud those parents are mine,
Feeling like I'm on cloud number nine.

Bethany Hale (12)
Pedmore Technology College, Pedmore

The Superstar!

I am famous, as you know
Do a concert, watch me go
Dancing, prancing around the stage,
Don't mess with me or you'll see my rage.

Do my own tea? I don't think so!
Butlers yes, others say no
Come to my house, you won't get in,
Guards will throw you in my waste bin.

My house is a mansion, good for me,
My huge house, it's just for three,
Go for a dip in my pool,
My neighbours think I'm so cool.

The world to me,
Is a little pea,
It is on my fingertips
Everyone loves my luscious lips.

My life is great,
I am proud
Look at me twice
And I'll shout out loud.

All my fans are special to me,
But all of that you can't see,
My parents, I love them dearly,
But that is shown very clearly.

Jodie Bostock (12)
Pedmore Technology College, Pedmore

How The World Must Seem For A Plant

There is a thud
Constantly getting bigger and louder
I wish I could crush that thing
Into powder.

I feel as though
There is an earthquake . . .

Argh! I'm getting flooded again
It feels like I'm in a lake
At least I have water to make food, but . . .

Making food is not that easy
But getting a creature is
Unluckily I can't speak
That language.

Oh no, I can see ants on me
How come everybody thinks
We're lifeless and have no senses
We're not those dead-ooking fences!

Do you know
The only thing that will never, ever
Make me run?
Is that big, beautiful sun!

Hopefully, my friend's
Having a better life that me in plant heaven
Huh! I still feel like I'm getting
Stabbed with a knife.

Every night, this creature puts me in these dungeons
And in that cage on my roots
Which I'm in 24/7!
I always pray to the Lord to take me away
In that creature's vehicle, the Ford.

Finally, today I see light in that Ford . . .
It's an angel to take me to plant heaven
I knew I was to die soon,
I have been flooded loads of times!

I don't understand, they're putting me in that big black bag
And now in that truck
I'm getting squished and squashed
And my bits are being scattered.

I think this is the end
Which always happened to my loyal friend
Life for a plant
Is a knife through the stem!

The creatures,
You treat them with oxygen
And this is how you get treated . . .

Suhail Ali (12)
Pedmore Technology College, Pedmore

Ladybird

Ladybird, ladybird,
I'm small and red,
With five little black spots,
On my head,
I flutter my wings all day,
In the fright blue sky,
As high as I can fly,
I'm as quiet as a mouse,
When I'm entering my house.

Ladybird, ladybird,
Everything so big,
Like that stick over there,
Watch out! Be careful!
I wish I were as big as an elephant,
I would walk on people who try to with me,
Oh, I wish I were big like an elephant.

Ladybird, ladybird,
What pretty colours I have,
I'm red with black spots, oh yes I am,
But also quite lonely,
As I flutter my way home.

Sophie Radford (13)
Pedmore Technology College, Pedmore

The World Through Someone Else's Eyes

Everything seems to go by in a flash
Giving things a quick bash
Pouncing on my prey
Definitely in May on a summer's day
Leaving my prints behind me
I go off to look for my tea
Building my home for me and my family
I sprint across the country
Feeding me and my cubs
I go off to find water as there are no pubs
Just to find a good spot to rest
But first, I always give it a test
Off I go for my morning run
But I always meet someone with a gun
Pointing it at me
I run for my life!

The cheetah!

Ryan McCullagh (11)
Pedmore Technology College, Pedmore

Famous Person

My name you all know,
Wrapped up in my show,
I parade round like a superstar,
Twinkle, twinkle, I've got far.
From a little girl,
To a strawberry twirl,
In a mad, mad world,
But my hair will always be curled.

'Cause this is my world,
Nobody else's,
Get out, leave,
Baby's starting to teethe.

Crying, dying in other countries,
People throwing different punches,
Nobody cares do they?
There's something wrong.

People getting married,
I'm on my own,
People in restaurants
And I'm not,
Because the world is cruel,
People say it,
It's true,
You should know.

My job is to rap,
I need a nap,
Parties all night,
I always see a light,
Lead me to it,
Just lead me to it.

Stardom is my life,
My friend has a knife,
Think, pause, what' she gonna do?

People applaud but it isn't an act,
I know the fact,
She's dead,
She killed herself.

Police investigate her suicide,
But I just tell them she died,
Form a nervous breakdown.

Now, it's funeral day
Nothing to say,
But shut up,
Go already.

She's gone,
Bye.

Molly Harper (11)
Pedmore Technology College, Pedmore

The World Through Somebody Else's Eyes

How the world must be for a famous star,
Rich and popular,
That's all they are.

Singing, dancing and drama too,
All they want are fans
Like me and you.

Style and money
They've got the lot,
I wish I had it all,
A never-ending pot.

How I wish to be a popstar,
I know I would go far!

Alexandra Steventon (12)
Pedmore Technology College, Pedmore

I Should Like To . . .

I should like to touch
A meteorite
I would like to hear
The clouds clashing together
I would like to touch
The fur of a polar bear
I would like to feel
The surface of the sun.

Matthew Knowles (12)
Pedmore Technology College, Pedmore

I Should Like To . . .

I should like to touch
The clouds
I should like to hear
The rays of the sun
I should like to see
Deep, deep down into the sea
I should like to smell
The heavens
I should like to taste
The spider's venom.

Kirsty Parker (12)
Pedmore Technology College, Pedmore

I Should Like To . . .

Touch the shiny star
Touch the rainbow
Touch the sky
Hear aliens
Smell frightened rabbits
Touch the moon in the sky.

Ali Hussain (12)
Pedmore Technology College, Pedmore

Environment

The environment is very nice
Except when there's litter
It ruins everything around us
If people pick up litter
The world wouldn't be polluted
The ozone layer wouldn't be touched
Everybody would be safe
But people don't listen!

Luke Jefferies (12)
Pedmore Technology College, Pedmore

My Dad In Heaven

I look down upon them
And see them sad and lonely
I think of all the good times
I had with them
But then I look back
And see my children are crying to me
I love them all to bits
I'm sorry I wasn't a good dad to you
But I can never change and be with you
Just remember, I love you both to bits
And you will always be in my heart
Forever and ever!

Kerri Louise Garbett (13)
Pedmore Technology College, Pedmore

Having A Home And Family

Having a roof over my head
Having a family love me
Always having a cosy bed
Having yummy great tea
Watching the news
Of the young children who are poor
We always get the blues
Sad and misery throughout us all
What a useless law
People are very alone
Always in rags
Skinny as a bone
Never got bags
Food, food, never an unused word
Drinks, drinks, not enough
There's a herd of them
And it's really tough
For me it's easy
For them it's hard
Saying I'm alone
Is not as bad as it is for them
I have a phone
I have a family
I love the outside world
And I take it with pride
There's always a sticky bend
But for them it could be
The end.

Tammy Cox (13)
Pedmore Technology College, Pedmore

Bullies

Bullies are very sad
And they can be really bad,
Always stand up to them,
They can be really dumb,
They had my lunch
And they gave me a punch,
I wanted to go home,
But they didn't let me go alone,
They pushed and shoved
And they made me feel . . .
Unloved!
Bullies think they're it,
Top of the class,
No one can stand against them,
If you mess with one,
You are going to have to deal with all of them,
They smoke, most of them,
They've got gangs and one leader.

Anjeela Wakeel (13)
Pedmore Technology College, Pedmore

Let Youth Be Heard

I want to mean something to the world,
I want my voice to be heard,
Make a change if I can,
Put smoking forward to ban,
But we are known as youth
And to tell you the truth,
We are known as bad, bad yobs
We are horrible to those snobs,
How are we supposed to change?
They shout, 'Yobs!' we shout, 'Strange!'
Can't they just see what the world means to me?
I would do anything to throw bad things away,
Be prime minister for a day,
I would ban, I would stop,
Just put us to the top,
Please make my voice heard,
Or just listen to those nerds.

Chelsea Savoy (11)
Pedmore Technology College, Pedmore

Confidence

As I enter the stage, my heart starts to beat,
I stand there staring, feeling the heat,
A million eyes flash at me,
A vast array of faces is all I can see,
I start to run towards the door,
Becoming breathless more and more.

The lights hit me, the music plays,
I suddenly snap out of my disastrous daze,
I begin to sing and realise,
What's the point in trying to hide?
I now understand that all you need,
Is *confidence,* so just believe!

Chloe McMurray (12)
Pedmore Technology College, Pedmore

Dream

On a cloud so fluffy and soft,
Like a giant pillow, brand new from the shop,
Floating in the air,
With nothing there,
Oh, I feel so alone, but what do I hear?
Oh, I hear singing getting near.

As I opened my eyes I saw little men,
One came up to me and said, 'Hi, my name's Len,'
I asked, 'What are you people and what are you doing in my dream?'
Then Len said, 'We are the letters of the alphabet,
Sorry we seem so mean.'

'I'm Rocket,'
'I'm Star,'
'I'm Apple,'
'I'm . . .'

Then Len clicked his fingers,
With a flash, I was back in my room in a dash,
I still remember that night,
When I had a bit of a fright.

I told my dream to everybody I knew,
They all said I needed help and made me see Mr Loo,
For what I knew I was OK,
As calm as a lake.

Lydia Campbell (12)
Pedmore Technology College, Pedmore

Football!

Wolves vs West Brom
Get in West Brom!
Chelsea vs Man City
Go Chelsea!
Baggies vs Derby
Who is going to win?
Baggies, of course!
When West Brom won vs Wolves
I was so happy
Better luck next time, Wolves!
Watch out Derby
The Baggies are coming
And we are going to win!
But if we lose
All of that practise for nothing
And the whole of the Midlands
Will go quiet!

Eloise Mount (13)
Pedmore Technology College, Pedmore

A Dark Night

I stand here in this dark, dark world
And all I can see is the darkness unfold
I try to think of apple pie
But a man comes along, so I say, 'Hi.'
Over the road there's a woman dying
This place really is goosepimplyfying!
So what in the world has become of us?
We who are living in Monstropolus
What do you think is happening here?
Because this place is full of fear.

What is happening in this dark, dark place?
There's a knight going round, swinging a mace
He chops off heads and hides them in a tree
Oh my gosh! He's on a killing spree!
Ghosts are flying
People are dying!

Liam Taylor (12)
Pedmore Technology College, Pedmore

The Big View

I stand here in this perfect land,
And wonder if it really is that great and grand.
The youth of today need to stand and speak,
And try to make an impact when our future looks bleak.
The wars that are happening, disasters and deaths.
We need to put an end to it, step by step.
The rivers are polluted, the tips are full.
We're killing the environment and making it dull.

I think of the great memories and times I had.
The deep of the ocean, they're so great, they're mad.
The amazing coloured sunset descending from the sky
Behind the perfect mountains where all the birds fly.
We need to have a good long think, *what's happening here?*
Our world is dissolving into fright and fear.

Adam Hodges (12)
Pedmore Technology College, Pedmore

In The Dark

Peering through wide eyes
Into a dark place
With large ears hearing every sound
Small voices bouncing off their shadowy homes
Their time had begun
They came to life
With sharp teeth like small knives
The night calls them
They must escape
They're ready to hunt
Three, two, one
The bats take flight!

Amy Timmins (12)
Pedmore Technology College, Pedmore

Hell!

He-e-elll! He-e-elll! Hell!
Burning fire,
Oozing blood,
Flowing through a river
And thick as mud,
The Devil awaits there,
With an evil tongue
And fiery hair.

Your head will come off,
You'll look like a dummy,
You'll be saying,
'Oh, where's my mummy?'
Your feet will smell,
Your belly will explode,
You'll look like a terrible, treacherous toad.

You will choke as you inhale, hot, hot steam,
You'll go deaf as you hear piercing screams!
Oh, cruel world!
What have I done to deserve this?
I have learnt my lesson,
Oh, do have mercy!

Zarcur Dard (12)
Pedmore Technology College, Pedmore

From The Beginning To The End

Have you ever wondered where you came from?
Well, just you come along
And sit down in your favourite chair,
While we tell you in a song.

You first started as a fertilised egg,
Then you grew into an embryo with arms and legs,
You were born as a baby, with a nappy and a cot,
Then you turned into a child, when you'd grown a lot.

When you were a teenager, you went all moody
And to your friends and family, you spoke quite rudely,
On your thirteenth birthday, you started to smoke
And you stopped drinking apple juice and diet Coke,
You switched instead to booze and you took drugs too,
Then you started bringing boys home, well, that's nothing new.

Next, you were an adult and you got a job,
But then you got sacked and you turned around and sobbed,
You took to dealing drugs, just to make a little dosh
And got married to a madman, just cos he was posh,
You used him for his money, then you left him on his own,
I'll bet you any money, he's still sitting there alone.

Now you're an old-age pensioner,
You're as wrinkly as a prune
And you wonder what is life, as you stare up at the moon,
Then suddenly, you know, as you gaze up at the sky,
Your life will never end, not even when you die.

Mary Senier (12)
Pedmore Technology College, Pedmore

Street Crime

Youth of today,
Most of them locked away,
Lots and lots of street crime,
Fighting till the end of time.

So many yobs,
None of them with jobs,
Too busy fighting and vandalising the park,
They say their 'crew' is making their mark.

A 'crew' with a leader called Blade,
He tells them to cause a big raid,
They shout, 'Here come the cops!'
As they steal from the shops.

What is happening on the street?
This most certainly isn't a treat,
It happens all through the year,
Can people not hear?

Aneisha Jones (12)
Pedmore Technology College, Pedmore

A Bad Memory

It was a dark, but starry night,
The forest was beginning to freak me,
It was getting darker and darker, later and later,
I could hear rustling in the bushes
And a face was staring at me.

I began to run, in the opposite direction,
There was someone after me, I knew,
The face was as pale as a ghost,
Almost as bad as mine,
I heard it floating after me.

It must be a ghost, I thought,
There were no footsteps, only mine,
Getting faster and faster with every step,
Maybe they had lost me,
I turned around quickly, not stopping just in case,
It was in the bush, I could see.

And then I realised,
I ran back quickly to the bush,
I scrambled around in the thorny brambles,
I pulled it out,
The scary, monstrous, horrendous, pale face,
Was a balloon!

Gabby Harris (12)
Pedmore Technology College, Pedmore

This Is My Life

Turning back time
Sounds impossible
I wish I could
I'll always regret that day
Late in April
Walking home
Little old lady
With walking stick
Seemed . . .
Vulnerable
Too vulnerable
Pulled a fiver
Out of her pocket
I really regret this
I killed her for a fiver
She gave it to me
Didn't want any trouble
Without thinking
Pushed her in the road
Splat!

As I sit writing this
The prison guard knocks on the bars
I look up
He has a bowl of mushy slop
All we get
All day
Every day
Behind bars - convicted of murder
Still here after seventeen years
The rest of my life to come.

Joanne Kay (11)
Pedmore Technology College, Pedmore

Away With Words

We got up very early
The lane was quiet and still,
I was wrapped up in a nice warm coat
I didn't want to get a chill.

It was 5 o'clock in the morning
My case was packed and ready,
We all got into Dad's car
Mom, Dad, Brad, me and teddy.

We travelled to the bus stop
Outside Dudley zoo,
There were lots of other people
And we joined the queue.

A coach pulled up beside us
As we put our cases on,
I climbed up all four steps
And sat down next to Mom.

We travelled for a long time
Along the motorway,
We reached the Channel Tunnel
It took nearly all day.

When we reached the other side
It was still a way to go,
Where were we going?
I still didn't know.

When the journey ended
We arrived in the dark,
Then I suddenly realised,
We were at Disneyland Theme Park.

I couldn't wait till morning
To meet Donald Duck,
I knew it was worth it
The long journey we took.

Ellis Hodnette (12)
Pedmore Technology College, Pedmore

Abduction!

It was a dark and scary night,
I was surrounded by trees,
In a blink they weaved around me,
Forming an archway as long as the eye could see,
I followed the archway, what would you have done?
The most foolish thing I ever thought of,
For when I got to the end it was unbelievable,
Something you could only dream of,
I felt faint as the image stuck in my mind,
Just kept appearing time after time,
As quick as a flash, there was nowhere to run,
I kept fretting whilst trying to keep a clear mind,
The feeling inside was absolutely horrendous,
I just couldn't control myself,
I was a nervous wreck and didn't know what to do,
I tried every direction, but there was nowhere at all,
They were closing in, whatever they were,
Their hands aiming and grasping my neck,
They took me in a complete black hole,
What were they? I didn't know,
Do you?

Sammie Pardoe (12)
Pedmore Technology College, Pedmore

Closer

I want a glass of water,
So I wake up in the night,
I open my door to see the kitchen set alight,
My mouth is gaped so wide,
The fire looks so alive,
The fire is rising and falling
Like the waves at the seaside,
It is like a monster from Hell,
I just cannot tell!
Its deep amber eyes stare at me with pain,
It feels so strange,
It's coming closer and closer . . .
Its teeth look so sharp,
It begins to cry out rivers of blood,
It looks like it's done no good,
Its heart begins to bleed,
What now stands before me is a demon,
It used to be a human,
Born into a world of chaos,
Neglected and chained,
Made into a sacrifice as a child,
Burnt to death, its ashes were piled,
It was then brought back to life as a creature of sorrow,
It's coming closer and closer . . .
I feel pain surging right through me,
I look down to see my heart, in the demon's hands,
I look up to see the demon's raging eyes burn right through me,
I open my eyes to be chained in a dark, dark hole,
It's coming closer and closer . . .

Laura Banks (12)
Pedmore Technology College, Pedmore

Fairies, Fairies Everywhere

Fairies, fairies everywhere,
In the corridor,
Up the stairs,
Fairies, fairies all around,
In the clouds or on the ground,
Pairs of twinkly toes and feet,
Of every fairy, its unique.

Fairies, fairies with pretty wings,
They are so magical,
They can do many things,
Like granting wishes
And taking teeth,
To a magical place,
Far beneath.

Fairies, fairies all around,
You never see them . . .
Not a sound.

Alice Nicholls (12)
Pedmore Technology College, Pedmore

Away With Words

Riots are raging out,
I can't see, I can only hear,
I'm blind, I don't know what to do,
Listening to the shouting and arguing,
I wonder what is going on,
People are moving from home to home,
I can hear the engines going back and forward,
Front doors slamming and falling down,
People are moving from home to home,
Gunshots and killings everywhere,
People just don't care,
I'm glad I'm in my bedroom,
Because I don't want to be one of them,
Staying in my bedroom,
I wonder what's going on,
Lonely by myself,
No one to keep me company,
I'm all alone.

Philip Huxley (12)
Pedmore Technology College, Pedmore

Life Goes On

Second by second,
Minute by minute,
Hour by hour,
Day by day,
Week by week,
Month by month,
Year by year,
We get older.

This is called growing up,
Not many people like it
But life goes on,
Today went fast,
Although I wanted it to last,
Life goes on.

Harry Till (11)
Pedmore Technology College, Pedmore

December Days!

I remember,
Some time in December,
When it was cold
And it always snowed.

The water stopped,
The whole place rocked,
It went dark,
In the middle of the park.

I was scared,
I ate the roll I'd prepared,
Then I went to my nan,
Who owned this wretched caravan!

I remember,
Some time in December,
When it was cold
And it always snowed.

Jack Deeley (12)
Pedmore Technology College, Pedmore

Life

I sit here listening to the news
Staring out the window
Staring into the window
Staring into the baby-blue lit sky and the grey cloud
As I see a bird fly by
I think to myself, *I wonder how a bird's life is planned?*
Were they made to fly
Flapping their wings as my life passes them by?
Watching TV now, thinking I can do this
And in my mind I see a horse galloping through the fields
Watching the blue sky as the clouds move south
I think and wonder, *if I were a horse,*
Would my life be as boring as it is now?
Would there be wars where men would die?
Women left to care for their kids and carry the death of loved ones?
I guess I will just have to find out through my journey in life.

Ashleigh Simpson (14)
Perryfields High School

Me

I was born in Jamaica where it is nice and hot
Now I've moved to England, my patois language has to rot
Sometimes I speak it to my mom
But when visitors come, my mother tongue has to run
Speaking a second style is hard
It's like opening my mouth and swallowing card
It never comes out right
It makes me seem like I'm not bright
One day I would understand this English thing
Walking round with gold teeth and silver bling.

Shalayna Hutchinson (16)
Perryfields High School

I Have A Dream

I have a dream to play for Wolves,
And kick a lot of footballs.

I have a dream to win all over,
All the way to Dover.

I have a dream to score
And to hear the fans roar.

I have a dream to play with Keogh,
I think he's great, he's my hero.

I have a dream to shoot
With my powerful boot.

I have a dream to scream when I score,
I'll keep on doing more and more.

I have a dream to be a legend,
All the way till I'm in Heaven.

Zach Howells (12)
Pool Hayes Arts & Community School, Willenhall

I Had A Dream

I had a dream,
All mine,
I didn't tell anyone,
But myself,
In my mind.

I dreamt that I would be,
A fantastic pop star,
Singing high and low,
Loud and quiet,
I would be . . . famous!

Hooray, I could be like
Rhianna,
Gwen Stefani,
Kylie Minogue,
Madonna!

Wouldn't it be great,
You never know . . .
You might see me soon!

Sarah Joynes (12)
Pool Hayes Arts & Community School, Willenhall

I Have A Dream

I have a dream, I have a dream,
To fly to the moon and back,
I have a dream, I have a dream,
To make all equal, white and black.

I have a dream, I have a dream,
To stop the world at war,
I have a dream, I have a dream,
That people must do more.

I have a dream, I have a dream,
To stop misery for all,
I have a dream, I have a dream,
That all mankind won't fall!

Ashley Jones (12)
Pool Hayes Arts & Community School, Willenhall

I Have A Dream

I have a dream,
Inside my head,
That comes to life,
When I go to bed.

I dream that I,
Can write a book,
That warms hearts
And doesn't suck.
Inspired by writers,
Far and wide,
That made you scared
And sad inside.

I dream that I,
Could sing a song,
Not too short,
Not too long.
Precise and perfect,
In a voice so sweet,
That could bring clapping people
To their feet.

I dream that I,
Can act for gold,
And melt the hearts
Of people cold.
Inspired by actors,
And huge stars,
That have bags of money
And swish cars.

I have a dream,
That I feel,
I can fulfil,
I can make real.
I am a mom,
And a wife,
And live a very happy life.
A husband and daughter,
As well as a son,
Inspired by all the parents
And all those to come.

Morganna Lewis (12)
Pool Hayes Arts & Community School, Willenhall

Ashley Tisdale

I have a dream . . .
Ashley Tisdale is the best,
She is better than the rest,
I want to be just like her,
When I am older, that's who I want to be.

She is a good actress,
A good singer,
She has released a CD,
That's what I am going to do.

I am going to be on TV,
I am going to be a singer,
I am going to release a CD,
I really, really want to be famous.

Oh my God, I'm on TV,
What should I do?
I have got loads of money
And everyone loves me.

I love to sing,
I love to dance,
I love to be on TV,
I love Ashley Tisdale when she inspires me.

That's who I want to be,
I really like her,
I hope you will like me when I become famous,
Please, please like me.

Nicole Thiara (12)
Pool Hayes Arts & Community School, Willenhall

I Have A Dream

I have a dream to be an actress like my sister
Sometimes she has a good look
She can be loads of things like . . .
A mum
A bride
A child
A princess
A queen

The main point is she is an actress
And I am proud to call her my sister

I have a dream, I have a dream
To be just like my sister when I am older.

Alana Klyvis (11)
Pool Hayes Arts & Community School, Willenhall

My World

The temperature is rising, each and every day
Stop polluting now, or we'll have to move away
The forests and the deserts, we need to claim them back
Plant loads of seeds and recycle waste and fat!

Madeleine's lost, Madeleine's gone!
We need to get her back and help her dad and mom
In China, oh China, the population is growing
One child per family, or you'll have to let them go and . . .

Children are starving, no water, no food
How would we live with no water or food?
Prince Harry wants to fight, but we don't want him to die!
But yet, all our sons have to fight, fight, fight!

The FA Cup, the Premiership too
Posh and Becks, Rooney's gone *coo, coo!*
The rumours are, Tony Blair has resigned,
Who will be next? Well, Gordon Brown's in line.

So what do you think of our world today?
Do you think it's good, do you think it's OK?
Personally, I'd like to change *everything*, like guns and hate
But we could do it all right, we could start again!

Sasha Stanley-Gaussen (12)
Shireland Colligate Academy, Smethwick

The World

People we love, we hurt
We sometimes even treat them like dirt

The world is such a dreadful place
I wish I could wrap it up in a soundproof case

Why so many wars?
Though many are puzzled about the cause

Sad ones cry with little hope
This just about helps them cope

Peace is what we need
Then all these sick ones we will feed

Their cries will turn to laughter
From now and thereafter

We will care for each other
Just like a loving mother

A lovely place the world can be
If only you'll open your eyes and see

I hope this dream will come true
But it's left up to me and you.

Nemeesha Patel (11)
Shireland Colligate Academy, Smethwick

My Poem

This is a poem about my world today,
How chaotic and exaggerated it is,
It is getting worse by the day.

Maddy, Maddy, the world has gone mad,
Maddy, Maddy, will you ever be found?

People are paranoid about being fat,
They are just silly and plain daft,
Starving themselves to be a size zero,
They think they're healthy, just like a super hero.

So! If you agree the world is going mad,
It's full of people good and bad,
So that's my poem of the world today,
Think about it nearly every day!

Grace Meah
Shireland Colligate Academy, Smethwick

My World

So he has named the date,
No more meetings and no more debate,
Goodbye Tony Blair and hello Gordon Brown.

Ten years at number ten,
All gone at the stroke of a pen,
Now is the time for someone else to wear the crown.

Did he lose?
Did he choose?
I guess we will never know.

So we wait,
For the date,
When the new Prime Minister starts his show.

Rameez Akhtar
Shireland Colligate Academy, Smethwick

My World

I sit down on my step,
Lift my eyes to the sky
To see the world.

Have you ever looked out over the world?
The people move like ants
In a wave

But they all have one thing in common . . .
Hope.
It turns the world and gets you up in the morning

When a child is lost, it's so easy to lose hope, but we don't,
We look at each other and try;
We do whatever it takes to sort it out

That's what keeps us going, like a wheel,
We don't stop until we have done everything we can,
Even then we don't stop hoping for them to be OK and come home.

When parents bury a child
It seems like there's no hope.
They have to find the words to say to the world
To stop it happening again.
So they bite their lips and do what they have to
And hope it works

They do interview after interview
And sit outside police stations waiting for a result.
They have news crews outside their door
And flowers from people they don't know,
But they smile and are grateful
Because if it just stops one more killing
It's all worth it.

We are all full of hope and dreams
That are so easy to break.
I think that if you work hard enough
Then they might come true

I hope one day I can do something that will change the world
Say a word that will ripple in an ocean of minds
Or find a place that no one has seen before

The world is full of scattered dreams that can change everything.

Eleanor Cann (12)
Shireland Colligate Academy, Smethwick

My World

My world is a violent storm
Rolling clouds of terror and despair
Stretch endlessly above me as I crawl along
Even my shadow is needlessly defeated
By the lack of glittering sunshine.

War crushes everything in its path
Tossing away humans like broken toys
Shattering happiness like a smooth, shining mirror
Love is stamped on by the foot of malice
And the burned remains of joy
Blow sadly across the stunted landscape.

Time chases both the rich and poor
Brings sorrow, unhappiness and death
Circling above the world like a raven
Waiting to swoop down and fly away with people's hearts
Time is stronger than the sun
More unpredictable than the sea
It is eternal.

Greed hungrily devours our planet
Sneaking slyly into our vulnerable minds
Possessing us in such a way that we are almost inhuman
Forcing us to crave more and more
Greed's buddies; thieving and trickery
Are here to lend a hand
Encouraging you to steal and lie to people
When they need your help most.

But war doesn't exist when there is nothing to destroy
And time also brings happiness and joy
If there is no value, then greed is no more
And, best of all, we have hope.

Like a bright, glittering butterfly
Hope glides through the iron-grey clouds
Buffeted this way and that by the vicious winds
But still shining brightly to lead the way
In my stormy world.

Minerva Pawsey (12)
Shireland Colligate Academy, Smethwick

My World!

Some people on Earth are angels,
Whereas some are like devils.
People sit and wear bangles,
Not with a care for the world.

So many things happen, like wars,
World War One and World War Two.
So many people die,
While the cows go *moo.*

And right now, a little 4-year-old girl,
As she was called Madeleine, has been kidnapped.
Seeing as no one was seated at their window sill,
No one saw the kidnapped girl.

I don't mind if anyone else hates it,
But I love my world a lot.
For whatever the weather is,
We can wear gloves for the cold
And sunglasses for the heat.

But still, I love my world so, so, so.

Sarasuati Jaiswal
Shireland Colligate Academy, Smethwick

My World

My world has some really beautiful places
Some I've never even seen
It also has some really horrid, gloomy places
So dark and miserable and mean

Life comes and goes without a warning
We just thank the god that we believe in
For waking us up in the morning
We try not to think about all those
Who have no shelter, no food or water
They barely can afford life itself
Which can be taken by the strike of a knife
They just pray and fight, for their miserable lives

Seeing the sun setting, your children playing
Knowing that they're safe and sound
Not thinking about the other side of the world
Begging strangers for just a few pounds

My world has some really beautiful places
Some I've never even seen
It also has some really horrid, gloomy places
So dark and miserable and mean!

Gratitude Katega (11)
Shireland Colligate Academy, Smethwick

My World

Beady little eyes of Neptune gaze, upon the minute Earth
Seeing how the Earth works using nature, water, oxygen

Nature, the gentlest mother
Impatient with no child
The feeblest of the most wayward
Her admonition mild

Water here, water there
Water is everywhere
But due to our carelessness
Water may be extinct

Oxygen is what we breathe
What we use to have fun
Oxygen is what we need
To live our life to the extreme

But now Neptune is confused
What are those coming from the Earth?
Not guns, not thunder
But a flutter of coloured drums (fireworks)
That announce a fiesta, fiery needles
Softly they break apart
And Neptune swallows them whole

Beady little eyes of Neptune gaze
Upon the Earth to twitch
Making them look like owls
Hunting their prey.

Jagvir Garcha (12)
Shireland Colligate Academy, Smethwick

My World

What has our world become?
All over, dreams have been shattered.
But did anyone know,
That everyone mattered?

Look at this place,
Five soldiers killed on Saturday,
They may never have a chance
To see their children play.

Or worse . . .
A 12-year-old boy died,
Involved in a hit-and-run,
Obviously, many had cried.

Then comes a kidnapping of a four-year-old
Sweet, innocent girl named Madeline,
Kidnapped for what?
I hope they find her in time.

But what I want to see is people making a difference,
I don't want to see fake smiles covering sad faces.
I believe, and together we should believe,
That we can make our world a better place.

Harjit Jandu (12)
Shireland Colligate Academy, Smethwick

Why?

Why does the sky never fall, Mum?
Why can't we see what's above?
Why does Dad have no hair, Mum?
Why isn't this world full of love?

Why can't the moon be a disco ball, Mum?
Why is my sister so mean?
Why can't I be a chunk of cheese, Mum?
Why do I have to be so clean?

Mum, listen, why don't you?
You used to, but not anymore.
Why are you going all red, Mum?
Do you think I am being a bore?

Anisah Mahatay (11)
Sutton Coldfield Grammar School for Girls, Sutton Coldfield

Aaarrgghh!

7am, get up and go
Dragged out of bed like a yo-yo
I look in the mirror, what do I see?
Argh!
A red, huge, attention-seeking spot!
Oh, what a catastrophe!

Tonight's the school disco, I must look my best
But this red, huge, attention-seeking spot
Is causing a distress.
I get out my creams, Clearasil, Olay,
Slap on Nivea before it's too late.

I whip out my phone and start to text
'Help, my life's at an end!'
My friends look at me, eyes confused
'Where's the spot?' they say.
I tell them, I can't refuse,
'There, it's there!' I point at my nose
'No, there's nothing at all,'
I whip out my mirror and try to find it,
Then realise it was my sister
And her felt tip!

Saba Asam (12)
Sutton Coldfield Grammar School for Girls, Sutton Coldfield

Save The World

From the Arctic to Antarctica
The polar ice caps are melting
Cracking, crashing, splashing, flooding
We've got to save the world.

The factories in the city
Forever producing smoke
Smelly, dirty, polluted air
We've got to save the world.

Cars, buses, lorries, vans
Zooming by each day
Trains, planes, motorbikes, people
We've got to save the world.

Animals in the wild
Fish in the sea
Birds that are flying, lying, dying
We've got to save the world.

We must do something about it
Recycle if we can
Preserve energy and not cause pollution
So we can save the world.

Caroline Jeffery (12)
Sutton Coldfield Grammar School for Girls, Sutton Coldfield

Fair?

They treat me like a baby,
Or a toddler maybe,
Cos I'm just a teenage girl,
With a disability.

They avoid me in the street,
But that's just life for me,
Cos I'm just a teenage girl,
Who can't fit in the community.

They call themselves my best buds,
But they don't know the real me,
Cos I'm just a teenage girl
With friendship immunity.

They all think they're helping,
Crowding round me all day,
Cos I'm just a teenage girl,
Kept in captivity.

They know they are,
Yes, you definitely do,
So make life fairer,
For us with a disability.

Heather Jenkins (12)
Sutton Coldfield Grammar School for Girls, Sutton Coldfield

Regan's Poem

My name is Sarah,
I'm 8 years old,
Well, that's what they seem to say,
But since I'm locked in the cellar,
And it seems like forever,
I've never seen the light of day.

Beat up children, hurt them through!
Could that really be my parents' belief?
And did they know that one day too,
They would give a child oh, so much grief?

Well, maybe they were always right
And maybe I'm simply wrong,
So why is it that I don't get a fright?
They stay out, all night long.

A car pulls up and the front door slams,
The floorboards upstairs creak,
I turn around, he's standing there,
Yet all I can do is shriek.

I'm lying there, bruised and battered,
Red blood upon my right wrist,
I ache all over, feeling shattered,
Last thing I saw was that evil man's fist.

Oh Daddy, how could you hurt me so?
I *must* have done something wrong!
You kicked me, pulled me to and fro,
Well, it doesn't matter anyway,
I shan't be here for long . . .

Regan Barry (12)
Sutton Coldfield Grammar School for Girls, Sutton Coldfield

Try And Understand

I wake each morning dreading school,
I want to run away,
I have no friends, they all hate me,
I really loathe each day.

I'm silent in every lesson,
Although I speak aloud,
It's a burden hanging over me,
Like an enormous cloud.

At break I am called silly names,
Like 'stupid' and 'retarded',
I shrink into a corner
And feel so broken-hearted.

After school I go to a club,
With people just like me
And helpers who can understand,
People who really see.

My condition is critical
And that is just the start,
I have motor-neuron disease,
So try and have a heart.

Eleanor Knight (12)
Sutton Coldfield Grammar School for Girls, Sutton Coldfield

Mystical Paradises

Some say that we will see a light
A light that's so bright it will blind us
Then we'll find ourselves in God's great Heaven
Where we'll live in harmony for eternity.

Some say that we'll come to a shore
Where the sea meets up with the heavens
We'll get on a boat that will sail us to
There, the mystical paradise called Valhalla.

Some people think we won't die,
That a part of our soul lives forever,
In a vapour white form of our latter selves,
More commonly known as a spirit.

I say death is a dark, unknown void,
An endless space of black nothingness,
Where you're trapped to float, high above the Earth,
Until you will see the end.

But which one is right or which wrong?
Where did all these ideas come from?
Do we wish for these paradises of Heaven and Valhalla,
Just to think they're a better place after death?

Well, whichever one it is, Heaven or Valhalla,
The mystical paradise after death,
We'll all never know until the day we go,
You'll just have to wait and see!

Jennifer Cooper (12)
Sutton Coldfield Grammar School for Girls, Sutton Coldfield

The World

So many routes to take,
New opportunities,
Different ideas,
The path you want to take,
The direction you choose to travel in,
That's the world I see.

War and destruction,
Fights and unequal opportunity,
Families destroyed,
A divided world,
A world of two halves,
That's the world I see.

Everyone an individual,
Everyone with different thoughts
And different views,
Different opinions,
Living in one world,
That's the world I see.

Different countries,
Different races,
Different religions,
Different people,
Different, but the same in a way,
Living in one world and sharing,
That's the world I long to see.

Imogen Marriott (12)
Sutton Coldfield Grammar School for Girls, Sutton Coldfield

The World From My Point Of View

From my position,
The world has no time for me,
Only listening to those
With big voices and wallets.

From where I stand,
I'm irrelevant,
Just another citizen,
Who should be seen and not heard.

From my view,
We're ignored and humoured,
For curiosity
And new ideas.

Through my eyes,
I'm dismissed,
Waved off,
Passively.

Kerry Bird (11)
Sutton Coldfield Grammar School for Girls, Sutton Coldfield

A World That Matters

Open your eyes, take a look at the world
You'll be surprised
There is so much going on
There is laughter, there is shouting
There are cries
Lots of different people
Selfish, kind, greedy, generous
Those selfish ones
They don't make a fuss
Some people get everything
Some get none
The fortunate ones
They can have fun and be free to run
Not everything's perfect for all
We live in a world of arguments and war
We fight, we kill
And exactly what for?
The world is a place of joy, happiness
Anger and sadness
For most of us
We just want what's best
A world that matters
Matters to me
Matters to you
Matters to everyone.

Marissa Xam (12)
Sutton Coldfield Grammar School for Girls, Sutton Coldfield

What Difference Do I Make To This World?

Who am I to the world today?
Just another victim to get killed or abused,
Just another victim of abduction,
Just a youth seen as troublesome,
Or am I nobody?
Nobody who has no rights or life of her own,
Nobody who gets bullied or teased,
A waste of time and space in this cruel, cold-hearted world,
No, I am somebody.
Somebody who can make a difference to the world and how
                                                    it is today,
The violence, the crime, the hatred, the jealousy,
When will it stop? Never?
Sometimes you may feel the world is against you, but it's not . . .
Don't turn your back against it, join it, fight for what is right,
You know you can make a difference, so do something about it,
Don't sit there and give up, keep on trying
And you'll get somewhere in your life.
Remember, it's up to you on what you choose to do!

Jamilah Campbell (13)
Sutton Coldfield Grammar School for Girls, Sutton Coldfield

Destination

Screaming parents, I can't hear a thing,
Slamming doors right in my face,
What am I supposed to do with this thing inside me?

Bare feet, nowhere to go,
Cold floors, shivering body,
What am I supposed to do with this thing inside me?

It's raining now, my top is becoming see-through,
I can only see an alleyway on the side,
What am I supposed to do with this thing inside me?

It's all my fault, I shouldn't have been there,
I still dread the fact that the test was positive,
What am I supposed to do with this thing inside me?

Walking on an endless street,
People are sound asleep in their comforting houses,
What am I supposed to do with this thing inside me?

Finally, I think of a place to go,
High hilltops looking out onto the sea,
Now I know what I'll do with this thing inside me.

Walking even faster now,
Keen to just get there soon,
Now I know what I'll do with this thing inside me.

I am now at my destination,
Just realising my feet are bleeding,
Now I know what I'll do with this thing inside me.

Standing on the edge of a cliff,
Looking down into the water
Now I definitely know what I'll do with this thing inside me.

Palma Kashyap (13)
Sutton Coldfield Grammar School for Girls, Sutton Coldfield

Away With Words

Alone in the playground,
With nowhere to run,
Voices like daggers,
And they think it's fun.

Because I was chubby,
And a little bit short,
They taunted and teased me,
And never got caught.

But it all went away,
When I told a friend,
They suddenly stopped,
It came to an end.

As life carried on,
More people I met,
But all the bad feelings,
I'll never forget.

When I think of my friends,
They make me smile,
They are the people,
Who make life worthwhile.

Under the trees,
Listening to birds,
I write these memories,
Away with the words.

Anna Owen (13)
Sutton Coldfield Grammar School for Girls, Sutton Coldfield

War - A Child's Game

The game is easy, that's what you think,
You have ten players, they have six,
It's their turn to hunt and your turn to hide,
If they don't catch you, you'll stay alive.
They run after you with their imaginary guns,
If you're with someone on your team, you'll fight back,
You fake pain and death, it's really fun,
When you're only six, it's just a load of fun.
Twenty years later, you're playing the same game,
The opposite team are hunting you again,
You fight back for those that you love,
For those who, because of the enemy, are known up above.
But it's not as fun as when the guns were not real,
It's not as fun when they're made of steel,
You get hit and you fall to the floor,
It's not as fun as it was before.
You lie gasping, sodden with rain,
Thinking back to the time when there was no pain,
Thinking back to the time when you were only six,
Thinking back to the time when this was just a game.

Chloe Thompson-Haynes (13)
Sutton Coldfield Grammar School for Girls, Sutton Coldfield

Trying Too Hard

The world is a big place
And I am a small girl
A small girl in a big world
Trying to make a difference.

Wars, death, people in captivity
Running away from the law
Why are people changing the world
Making it turn worse?

People go missing
In natural disasters
In things you can't help
So why do people make it worse?

If people stand up for what they believe
Don't be pushed around by 'the man'
If we help each other and help the world
It'd be a better place.

One person has to start it off
I'd gladly save the world
From hopelessness and depression
I'll turn it all around.

I'll fight for what I believe in
I'll fight for what is right
I'll fight for my country
I know it'll be alright.

The world is a big place
And I am a small girl
A small girl in a big world
Trying to make a difference
Trying to make it better
Trying to make it right.

Laurel Windsor (13)
Sutton Coldfield Grammar School for Girls, Sutton Coldfield

What The World Has Become - Animal Cruelty

Hunting, killing, disowning and using
For our own human benefit
Many animals that we are still losing
Happen to become extinct by the minute

Soft, warm fur is being cut to bits
Innocent souls are abandoned in the cold, hard rain
Gentle reactions and big hearts, ripped to shreds
How can it be borne with all the pain?

Experiments, tests, projects and practical work
Mixing DNAs and harming animals
Frightening them out of their wits as they react and lurk
What will be achieved, despite the act of killing God's creatures?

Pets and animals are bleeding to death
Left on streets and dying every day
Being disowned and having their hearts broken
The hurt and anger for this cannot be paid

Another aspect is pollution in many places
Getting rid of them, but why?
They are living things too
As they take their last breaths or last couple of paces
Just because communication doesn't take place
In a way it does with each other in everyday life

Animals in their last tens
Pandas, polar bears, white tigers and many more
Treat animals how you would like to be treated
Just like the needy and poor

Finally, animals can also bring happiness and laughter
To a loved one
Stop and think, try to help make a difference
Globally, the world would end up in a disaster
Because the hurt and grief will never stop

It could happen any day or any time of the month
Just think . . .
Why animals, and why not us!

Ajit Kaur Sagoo (13)
Sutton Coldfield Grammar School for Girls, Sutton Coldfield

Life Through My Eyes

If we are God's creation, then so is every creature,
If this is so, then God is our teacher,
Colour, race and creed should be accepted,
If this is so, then why do others feel rejected?
The human ego, should be unused,
If this is so, then why do others feel abused?
We should be thankful, for all we've received,
If this is so, then why is money treated as human greed?
Peace and unity should be running through the water,
If this is so, then why is saying sorry torture?
Realisation of God, is the source of beginning,
Find this source and then start living.

Niharika Chadha (13)
Sutton Coldfield Grammar School for Girls, Sutton Coldfield

War

War is whatever,
Can't we stick together?
Maybe we don't realise,
The size
Of this matter.

Can't they just leave well alone?
If I were a soldier I'd want to stay home.
Instead, they think that war,
Will make it much better.
Why can't they just write a decent letter?

Frances Hancock (13)
Sutton Coldfield Grammar School for Girls, Sutton Coldfield

Our World

As time ticks by,
Cold will go,
Everything will be over.

Ice will be scarce,
The sun will be fierce,
Leaving us to find a way to live.

Polar bears will no longer be seen,
Water will swallow us up in big, large gulps.

Who's the culprit?
Who's to blame?
Is there anyone to take the shame?

Is it myth?
Is it a scare?
Does anyone really care?

So now there's time to change,
For the better,
To stop the world,
Coming to an end.

Recycle, give up,
Stuff you don't need,
For the better,
To restore happiness in the world again.

Areeba Tahir (12)
Sutton Coldfield Grammar School for Girls, Sutton Coldfield

My World

My world is a happy place,
Full of friends and fun.
Your world wears a sad face,
Ruled by a man with a gun.

My world has education,
Loving, safe and free.
Your world's a grieving nation,
Filled with gloom and poverty.

My world is successful,
Treating those who are ill.
Your world has little money,
You can't pay for a pill.

My world gives out money,
To help people like you.
Your world's getting better,
Because of what we do.

Natasha Branson (12)
Sutton Coldfield Grammar School for Girls, Sutton Coldfield

The World From My Point Of View

'News just in,
Global temperatures are rising',
I turn over the channel,
For that news is just not surprising.

Every other day or so,
Reporters warn us about global warming.
Who listens to it? Not many,
They just find it all rather boring.

I look up at the sky in mid-February
And see the hot sun blaze down,
This is not right, surely?
The seasons are swapping round.

'News report, thirty killed in a bank robbery',
I stare wide-eyed at the screen.
My mum just shrugs and carries on cooking,
How can you ignore it? It's just obscene.

I am one of the few who listen to the reports and sigh.
What can I do? Absolutely nothing.
Seniors ignore us, or even laugh,
They think our ideas are rubbish.

I am just too young to be heard,
But I will grow, we all do,
And maybe, just maybe, I can speak my thoughts,
And see how others feel too.

Rebecca Sheehan (12)
Sutton Coldfield Grammar School for Girls, Sutton Coldfield

Young Voices Want To Be Heard

Many people see us as mice
Who get in the way and cause trouble

But they don't realise
We are the generation of tomorrow
And they think we're there to cause them sorrow.

They hurt our feelings
Throw our dreams away
'You can't do it' that's what they say.

People wonder why
We have mood swings and tantrums
They say we complain and are insane.

They make us feel small
All these people
Teachers, aunties, uncles and all.

Sometimes we wish
We didn't exist
So many questions
We want to know
But when we ask
We're told to go.

One day I hope our voices
Will be heard
Our views seen and acted upon
Then they'll see the smile on our faces
Frowns and tears will be past cases.

Moyo Bajomo (12)
Sutton Coldfield Grammar School for Girls, Sutton Coldfield

The World From My Point Of View

Deep sinners, with open eyes
Steal, torture, take lives.
No second thoughts to change their minds,
Endless tries, needless finds.

Darkened days by hovering clouds
Among the shadowed light source.
Pitter-patter, pitter-patter is all I hear on the path
Forming a torrent, destroying all in its wrath.

How I miss those brushed streets,
Uncovered and seen.
Now no pair of eyes can peer through
Cans, papers, packets building up to you.

No souls are seen moving along the path,
No thought for living bodies.
All sheltered in vehicles, gas dispersing
Toxic smoke now gathering up, taking over, cursing.

Who knew water from above could harm?
Now fish, plants and trees without life.
Burning of fuels still persists
Warmer climates, greater petition lists.

Why does no one listen?
Why does no one care?
We're all the same, we're all human.
I see fighting and discrimination, for what?
Why not a polite conversation?

Will there be light? Will there be hope?
Will all enhance?
Will nature survive?
I'll have to wait and see
But that's life.

Haleema Mahmood (12)
Sutton Coldfield Grammar School for Girls, Sutton Coldfield

The World That We Live In

The world that we live in,
This world that we see,
Our life began and ended here,
But is it full of glee?

The news is never good,
Showing not the happy but the bad,
Is the world destruction,
Or is everyone just mad?

Pollution in our daily lives,
Getting in the way,
Factories, the greenhouse gas, where's the ozone gone?
But what if one of us had our say?

The inner city's such a big place,
It produces a lot of waste,
The countryside is vast and open,
Giving your life a new taste.

The seaside is the place to be,
The coast, the beach, the lovely, pleasant shore,
A place to relax in the sunshine days,
I wish there could be more.

Will all our problems be sorted,
Or is it too late?
Could life be different,
Or is this our fate?

Victoria Stephenson (12)
Sutton Coldfield Grammar School for Girls, Sutton Coldfield

The World

The moon tints the leaves with a swooning glow,
Beaming from the starlit sky,
Upon leaves that sprout from great wooden umbrellas,
Shadowing the barley and the rye.

A great blue canvas captures the sun
As it glides into view by noon,
The pearly-white clouds, the blossom of the day
Appear, but spoke too soon.

By evening, a shower is hammering down
And drowning the life below,
The leaves become dreary and the sun fades away,
Now, only the grey blossoms show.

The world is an ocean of many, many shells
And we take advantage of the ones we uncover,
Yet the ones that remain hidden beneath the waves
Carry many more secrets to discover.

Be it the shades of green from the common blade of grass
Or the dull, lifeless brown from the soil,
The colours of the world have so much to tell
As they pattern it with both tickles and toil.

So, take the world and use it to the full,
After all, it has so much to give,
From the natural resources to the countryside view,
Value it, for as long as you live.

Katey MacAllister (12)
Sutton Coldfield Grammar School for Girls, Sutton Coldfield

The World

Some people are starving, dying, crying,
Some people do not have the things they need,
Some people live in poverty,
All to do with politics, money, power.

Some people get paid millions,
Some people have too much,
Some people just play for money,
Why do they not give money away?

Lalita lives in Africa,
Lalita does not have a mother or father,
Lalita walks three miles for water,
Water which is muddy, unclean, unsafe.

Chardonnay is married to a footballer,
Chardonnay goes shopping every day,
Chardonnay turns on a tap and there it is,
Water which is so clean and fresh.

There are many charities,
Helping the poor and sick,
Not many people choose to help,
But think of a world that did.

People living a healthy life,
Everyone is equal,
No poverty, just peace all around,
A happy world of people.

Isobel Wilkinson (12)
Sutton Coldfield Grammar School for Girls, Sutton Coldfield

A World Of Contrasts (From My Point Of View)

The lesson has started
And as the teacher drones on,
I look out the window
And think, *what's going on?*

Somewhere people are fighting,
Countries going to war,
Gunfire splits the silence,
There is peace no more.

Elsewhere people are smiling,
Laughing and having fun,
Stretching out on beaches,
Relaxing in the sun.

Factories pump out poison,
Making people feel ill,
The smog gets thicker and thicker,
Closing in for the kill.

Birds are singing merrily,
Happy to be free,
Fish are swimming gracefully,
Through the deep blue sea.

While other people are starving,
Struggling through the day,
Rich and wealthy people,
Waste their money away.

From where I'm standing what I can see,
Are many people in need,
But some who could, choose not to help them,
Obsessed with money, full of greed.

Claire Guest (12)
Sutton Coldfield Grammar School for Girls, Sutton Coldfield

Our World

Pollution
Let's all have a resolution
Rubbish and litter found
Never forget to turn around

Throw things in the bin
You don't have a sin
You keep our world clean
And now you have seen

Look around with a beam
Is what you can dream
Unless you make a change now
And don't dare say how

All you have to do is not pollute
And then listen to the sound of a flute
Now you may see the sun shine
So come up to cloud nine.

Satkartar Chandan (11)
Sutton Coldfield Grammar School for Girls, Sutton Coldfield

Poem About War

People say it is necessary
But is it really?
Fighting all the time again and again
Innocent lives being shattered
Just for stupid reasons
Reasons that aren't even explained
You see it all the time on TV
You hope it will get better
But it is just getting worse.

Laura Sumner (13)
Sutton Coldfield Grammar School for Girls, Sutton Coldfield

Children Of Today

Today's world presumes every kid's like they see on TV
Well, that's where they're wrong
People need to give them a chance.

Some kids graffiti
Some kids bully
But some kids don't.

The world focuses on children who have bad behaviour
They don't focus enough on those children
Who do well at school.

Good children don't get noticed
Good children don't get praised
Good children get left out
Every single day.

Rachel Hawkins (12)
The City Technology College, Kingshurst

My Baby Guardian

Her eyes are like shiny pods that glisten in the night sky,
Trapping me with that innocent stare.
I feel her fur, as soft as a sponge cake,
And even like freshly cut grass.
Her ears, floppy like a rabbit's, bounce
As she trots towards me.

Licking her chops, like a lion watching its prey,
She lets out a whine that would melt the hearts of thousands.
Her concentration is broken by a knock on the door.
Her face is on suspicious alert,
Like a mother protecting her children.

Is it a killer?
She doesn't wait to find out -
She replaces her innocent baby face with a furious stare,
As scary as a pack of hungry wolves.
A deep rumble of a bark leaves her throat,
As loud as a deafening trumpet.
A lion protecting her property -
Protecting me.

I close my eyes and relax as I take in that beautiful smell,
Opening my eyes, I feel I'm at a beach,
The scent has been trapped in my throat,
Like a fly trapped in a web.

I know wherever I may be,
Her smell, touch, taste and sight will always be with me.

Kimari Strachan (12)
The City Technology College, Kingshurst

Snowflake Dog

My dog is a snowflake dog,
With eye-catching blue eyes.
His paws are like pillows
And his face is an angel.

His fur is a sea of silk,
His nose is a wet stone.
His smell when wet is an unbelievable stench,
But he is still my snowflake dog.

His bark is a lion's roar
And his bite is fatal.
But when he is called,
His stroll is stately and proud.

This is *my* dog!

Kieran Reilly (12)
The City Technology College, Kingshurst

The Amazing African Grey

My African Grey is a talking, walking, flying parrot.
The smooth grey feathers on his back
Are as ticklish as a cloud of dust floating up my nose.
He makes me wonder when he talks,
Sounding like a human with a blocked nose.

He violently flaps his wings,
Like the branches of a tree in a storm.
The red flicker of his feathers are emergency vehicle sirens.
Flying, he is like Concorde gliding through the air,
And like Spider-Man, he climbs his cage
Upside down and all around.

In the morning, he sings and squawks his songs,
Like a cat screeching on a rainy day.
The smell of his droppings fills the room,
Smelling like stale milk on a warm day.

He is my talking machine.

Lewis Jones (11)
The City Technology College, Kingshurst

The Seven Ages Of A Chip

Every chip is always interchangeable,
They go through that synonymous life,
First, you have the papoose seed,
With power and will inside it,
Shrouded away in ebonic mud,
Drinking its needed water.
Then we have the birth,
Where a mint life has come,
Growing and growing rapidly,
Peeking out of the ground.
Now we have the picking,
Of the opulent, big, brown spuds,
Sliced and diced till death
And no skin to be found,
Hacked up thin or fat,
You can choose the size:
The bare, cold carbo,
About to get discarded into the fryer.
Now we're on the fifth age,
Sizzling, seething and screaming,
Building up its majestic batter,
As man looks down upon them.
Coming near the end,
The chip is now sleeping, lifeless,
Waiting for the ketchup,
As it's put upon a plate,
The sauce is now splattered,
For all to luxuriate in,
Picked up and compressed:
Chomp it away!

Niall Coney
The City Technology College, Kingshurst

The Seven Ages Of A Crime Gang

All the world's a place of crime
And all the men and women are criminals.
They all play a part or do their work
And sometimes act like animals.
First is a boy sitting on a wall
Frustrated at his mother
For being manhandled and beaten
And acrimonious and other.
Second is talking to mates
They have an idea of what to do
For they were also being battered
And laid into.
Third, they form a little gang
And walk the streets at night
Stealing and beating people
Thinking of matricide.
Fourth, calling themselves convicts
They let other people join in
To rival other gangs
And to mark their territory.
Fifth, going to different areas
Annihilating other gangs
Committing burglaries and arson
All the Feds can do is hear the bangs.
Sixth is when it turns to horror
Misdemeanours, assassination
They call their territory 'Homicide City'
Their crime is far from imagination.
At the end, a plan goes wrong
The leader is caught, it's a nightmare!
The gang lies low waiting for the boss
But you can't escape one, shocking chair.

James Dowling
The City Technology College, Kingshurst

Best Boxer

My dog is a glistening snowman.
His elegant body
Flies majestically in the wind,
Following his ambition to be a performing horse.

His empowering voice echoes and spreads
Endlessly
As he marks his territory,
His rank - head of the pack.

As I touch him
His thin, flaky skin
Falls away in my hands,
Like melting snow.

He bounds up the garden
With ferocious speed.
His target found - a precious place,
A place that he calls home.

Samuel Bibb (12)
The City Technology College, Kingshurst

Monster Munch

M unching, sucking, horrible vampires
   That attack the living
O ctopuses, like creatures that drag sailors
   Into the waters of doom
N inety-foot dragons that burn brave knights
   To a crisp
S cary ghosts that haunt people
   And buildings alike
T rolls that hide under dark bridges
   Waiting to clobber and eat their next victim
E vil werewolves that terrorise villages
   Every full moon
R eally evil demons determined to destroy
   The entire world
S o we come to the monster, the worst of them all
   More smelly, horrible and dangerous than all the rest
   It is called . . .
   My little baby brother!

Alexander Brock (11)
The City Technology College, Kingshurst

Red

Red is the smell of smoke,
Erupting by a nearby volcano.
Red is giving you the taste of bitterness,
That's glued to your mouth.
Red is the touch of blood,
Gushing from the cut of a wrist.

Red is the sound of destruction,
Rushing from the valley of the damned.
Red is the sight of death,
Sweeping through a field of war and horror.
Red makes you feel an illness,
Marching through your defenceless body.

Liam Hehir (12)
The City Technology College, Kingshurst

The Snowman

The wind whistles across my face
I'm standing there cold
Throngs of people just stare
But no offer to take me in.

The sun comes out
I start to melt
I wish someone would take me in
Put me by a boiling fire.

I don't have a lot of memories
But the one I remember is the little girl
Who made me
She will always be in my heart
One day I'm here, the next I'm gone.

Chelsea Jones (12)
The City Technology College, Kingshurst

Christmas Time

At Christmas, carollers are singing,
Lots of children are playing,
Mothers are shopping,
And priests are praying.

When it comes to the last few days,
Mothers are rush, rush, rushing,
Trying to do their best,
Cooking, cleaning and brushing.

And when it comes to the big day,
Children unwrap their presents,
Mothers are happy for their children
And feel sorry for some poor peasants.

Siana-Rose Crawford (12)
The City Technology College, Kingshurst

Best Christmas

The snow fell on my face as it blew from the open window
My eyes popped open as I knew presents were downstairs
I raced into my mum's room and she got straight up
We ran downstairs to the tree
All my family were waiting for me
Presents wrapped up in Christmas paper shining there
My family passing presents and helping me tear
As we opened each present, my face lit up
Clothes, make-up and a little teddy bear cup
It was the best Christmas.

Shannon Kavanagh (12)
The City Technology College, Kingshurst

Happy Birthday

Everybody needs a birthday
Even if you're ten, fifty or even a hundred
It's a special day
You're the centre of attention
No one can ignore you
Happy birthday
Presents are stacked up high
It's like Christmas
But you're the only one getting presents
You rush downstairs
There's a twinkle in your eyes
And a big smile on your face
Happy birthday
Tomorrow it will be all over
Enjoy it while you can
It will just be a distant memory
Happy birthday!

Hollie Rodgers (11)
The City Technology College, Kingshurst

Best Friends

When a girl cries
All she needs is them
They are her true best friends
They are by my side every single day.

They are all I need
When I am happy or sad
Always making me laugh.

Best friends are like angels, only real
They stand by me and I stand by them
Like true friends should
Without them I am nothing.

I'll be their best friends
Till the day of my death
We shall stay best friends forever
To my very last breath.

Tahlia Banks (12)
The City Technology College, Kingshurst

Happy New Year!

The stars are bright
In the corner, the tree is shining light.

Everyone is ready,
Excited for a new year.

People are out on the town,
Singing and making a sound.

Santa came with new toys
Children with big smiles on their faces.

The new year is here, so enjoy it!

Eleanor Lane (12)
The City Technology College, Kingshurst

My Bedroom

Here I am sitting here
Getting myself into gear.

My bed invites me to lie down
I put on a smile, not a big frown.

I fall asleep for lots of hours
Probably dreaming of colourful flowers.

I'll never leave the room
Till I really have to go.

It's so special to me
No one else needs to know.

I eat there, I sleep there
I do everything I can there.

That probably explains
Why I don't let anybody in here!

Jadene Weldon (12)
The City Technology College, Kingshurst

At Grandma's House

Sitting in my living room, smells like roses
My grandad's taking pictures while I do poses.

Grandma's making tea, I get the cookies, cheerful as can be
Singing and dancing around with me.

'Let's have a party,' as my sister said
'No, no, no, off to bed.'
Jessica moans as she always does
Screaming and shouting and causing a fuss.

Playing with cards, shuffle, shuffle
Grandad cheats, what a kafuffle!

Seating and eating sweets from the tin
Grandad nicks one when I'm not looking.

Pepper and Reafy snoring their heads off
I can't hear the telly, then I get told off.

Grandma says it's time for bed
To go to bed and rest my head.
I sneak up the stairs past my sister's snoring head
Grandma says, 'Don't forget ted.'

Thank you for reading my poem
Mommy says, 'It's gold and jewellery.'

Alexandra Daykin (11)
The City Technology College, Kingshurst

The Pirates' Den

The sea waves went *crash*
As I was swallowed inside,
I had to go back, when in came the tide.

That night I'd never seen such a starry sky,
It looked even better than apple pie.

The sand came alive, as it danced in the wind,
I was sunbathing, so to the ground I was pinned.

Forever, I wished I could lie on the floor,
As hot as fire,
If I said that I wanted to leave, I would be a liar.

Louis Herbert (12)
The City Technology College, Kingshurst

Iraq

Colonel's screaming here and there,
The suicide bombers don't really care,
People dying in the midnight hour,
Whilst suicide bombers start to feel power.

Children fleeing up and down,
When people die, dogs start to howl,
Tears running down helpless faces,
Army are dying from all the races.

When gunshots are fired,
People perspire, thankful it's not them,
Shooting and burning,
Where the blood is churning,
In the street where people walk.

Young people are injured,
Helping each other,
When the only people worried,
Are their mothers.

We should show more care for those
Wasted lives,
People need anxiety
To show more care.

Jack Grant (12)
The City Technology College, Kingshurst

My Favourite Place

My favourite place,
Is not away,
I'd rather stay at home,
For I'd rather be with my family
Than a place like Russia or Rome.

My favourite place,
Is not at school,
Though it holds us all together.
I like to stay
With my friends each day,
Then we'll stay friends forever.

My favourite place,
Is in my home,
When I'm comfy in my bed.
I turn off my light,
Every night
And then I rest my head.

Lauren Sadler (11)
The City Technology College, Kingshurst

Football Finals

Here we are on the way to the game,
If we win we're in the Hall of Fame,
If we lose we're in the Hall of Shame.

Here we are in the quarter finals,
It all kicks off with Athletico Rhinos,
The referee stops the game,
Another year till the Hall of Fame.

Here are AFC in the finals,
Still against Athletico Rhinos,
If we win we'll be in the cruise,
If we lose we'll be just like the blues.

Kieran Gould (11)
The City Technology College, Kingshurst

My Favourite Place

T imid sound of the birds
H orror of the crashing waves
E verlasting flow of water

S unshine always shining
U nique and lovely
N ice and sweet
N atural and cool
Y oung and pretty

B eautiful and bold
E xciting and fun
A lways under the sun
C alm and collected
H appy and great

Look at the first letters of each sentence
What do you see?

Thomas Murphy (11)
The City Technology College, Kingshurst

A Secret I Know!

There is a secret I know,
One that I'll never show to you.

A secret I've lost,
A painful cost.
A secret I've lost,
And I've turned into frost.

A new secret I've found,
I'm proud as can be,
A new secret I've found,
One quite loud.

When it's wet and windy outside,
I hop there and hide.
When it's dry and hot outside,
I stay there and hide.

The secret I treasure,
Has trees that wave like a feather.
The secret I treasure,
Has wind that howls through the night
And gives me a fright!

The secret I know,
Is one that I'll proudly show.

Can you keep a secret?

Harry Charles (12)
The City Technology College, Kingshurst

Swimming Pool

Wet and noisy as I pull up
To my favourite swimming pool.
Slides and dives,
Excitement and cries.
Here I am at my favourite swimming pool.
Fun and laughter,
Relaxing mums,
Nervous people on the diving boards.
Here I am at my favourite swimming pool.
Packed to the brim,
Hardly anywhere to swim.
Here I am at my favourite swimming pool.
As the chlorine hits my throat,
I jump up with a splash.
Here I am at my favourite swimming pool.
Relaxing mums,
Cheerful dads,
Determined grandparents,
Playful kids.
Here I am at my favourite swimming pool.

Kayleigh Bricknell (12)
The City Technology College, Kingshurst

My Favourite Place

My favourite place is warm and cosy,
But my big sister can be a bit nosy.

My favourite place has my favourite things,
Sometimes I feel a bit sad to leave.

When I get home, I lie on my bouncy bed,
But sometimes I wonder, am I really dead?

Every day I leave my place for school,
Which I don't think is cool.

Sometimes I wish I could stay in my room forever,
But I can't do that, never ever.

'Home sweet home'.

Sometimes I go to my room for a groan,
But sometimes I just moan!

My room is the best,
Better than the rest!

My favourite place is warm and cosy,
But my big sister can be bit nosy.

The door welcomed me as I entered slowly,
The light through my window shone brightly.

My room is built just for a king,
That's why it's got my favourite things.

I closed my door with a bit of a bang,
Then all of a sudden I began and sang.

'Home sweet home,
Home sweet home.'

Andrew Morris (12)
The City Technology College, Kingshurst

Benidorm

Walking up the pathway, I am starting to sway
My ears start to burn, so I turn away
The sun is beaming at my head, I feel rather dead
I get to my apartment, I need to make my bed
The swimming pool is open, I might jump in to get cool.

Mikey Jarvis (12)
The City Technology College, Kingshurst

My Favourite Place

The lovely, colourful beach, a great place to be
The beaming hot sun gleaming on the sparkling sea
All you can see is the soft, blue sea swaying
And the sound of the little children playing
All the different colours, so many things to see
All the tropical drinks, flavours, shapes and colours
Blue, green and purple, so many colours to see
A lovely place to be singing and dancing by the sea
Walking on the dusky, yellow sand, watching the blue sea flow by
A wonderful place to be, sitting here by the sea.

Lindsey Peach (12)
The City Technology College, Kingshurst

My Favourite Room

L is for love, the main part of this room
I come here after school and relax very soon
V is for visits, we have many in here
I like it when family and friends are near
N is for nights we watch TV on the sofa
G is great fun we have there

And

D is for downstairs where this room is placed
I n warmth we sit, eat and taste
N is for nights we eat our meals here
I is for inside where I like to be
N ot forgetting the fun when watching TV
G is for get-togethers we host all around

This *room* is the best, no better to be found.

Amy Robinson (12)
The City Technology College, Kingshurst

My Little Sister In Spain

In Birmingham airport,
On the way to Spain,
Can't wait to see my swimming pool again.

In Spain it's as hot as an oven,
The pool is as cold as ice,
There are lots of cats to keep away the mice.

When I'm there I'm happy,
Until my sisters are snappy.
I'm in my bikini relaxing with my Martini.

Daishia Holmes (12)
The City Technology College, Kingshurst

Fashion Is Fashion

Fashion is what you wear and the way you do your hair
Don't worry if you're not pretty
Don't worry if you're not slim
Just throw your clothes out of your drawers
And chuck them in the bin
Now it's time to go on a shopping spree
With Sophie, Paige and Tee
Just look around the shopping mall
And see what you can see
They tried something new
Instead of old T-shirts and old jeans
They looked around for dolly shoes
Which were as fashionable as can be
They tried on some gorgeous tops
And some leggings to match too
They're nearly ready to pay for it
And go and party, *whoo-hoo!*
The night has come to have some fun
They look like shining stars in the sky
Later when the party ended
They said to three boys goodbye.

Tisa Carroll (12)
Tividale Community Arts College, Tividale

What Am I?

I'm boring and dull
I keep all your stuff
I don't like the dust
Have a guess
I knew you didn't know
I come in loads of colours
I keep your books
And things you need
I have loads of space
I might not be nice
But I keep your room clean
Can you guess
What I am?
A box.

Christopher Bagley (12)
Tividale Community Arts College, Tividale

All My Mates

There's Alice who I have a laugh with
And there's Leah who acts like a div.

There's Jess who's cute and small
And Sophie who's quite tall.

There's Andrea who's really funny
And there's Dipsaloo who's coming to get you.

My friends forever.

Emma Swift (12)
Tividale Community Arts College, Tividale

What Am I?

What am I?
I am very tall
Like a block of flats
What am I?
I wave through the air
Like an aeroplane
What am I?
I have long roots
Like plants
What am I?
I am a tree.

What am I?
I am soft to walk on
Like comfy carpet
What am I?
I can be any sort
Like rocky sand
What am I?
I am a pit of sand.

What am I?
I protect things
Like a guard dog
What am I?
I go around a garden
Like a wall
What am I?
I am fencing.

Kirsty Pilsbury (12)
Tividale Community Arts College, Tividale

Who Am I? What Am I?

Sitting in my cot
With what seems like a million eyes glaring at me
Like I'm a bucket containing a billion pounds
Who am I? What am I?

Unable to speak to tell these eyes to stop glaring at me
I have no control over my limbs
I have no control over my food
Who am I? What am I?

Some see me as a jewel, unable to lift a finger
Some see me as a peasant stinking up the place with my
                                    uncontrollable puke

I don't even know who I am
I don't even know my name
But there's this lady
This caring young lady
Who keeps on calling me David
David, my sweet little baby David
Who am I? What am I?
I have no idea.

Atang Ncube (12)
Tividale Community Arts College, Tividale

What Am I?

I'm hard, yet soft
I'm fast and smooth
I'm any colour, any brand
Juice me up and keep me clean
And take me where you will find your dream
I can blast out your song
I can store your things
I've got a system that deletes the pong
What am I?
A car.

Joe Harris (12)
Tividale Community Arts College, Tividale

Who Am I?

I'm small
Who am I?
People are scared of me
Who am I?
But I am scared of them
Who am I?
I live in damp places
Who am I?
I like to be let free
Who am I?
I have eight legs
Who am I?

Manraj Dhinsa (12)
Tividale Community Arts College, Tividale

What Is Happening?

What is happening?
I feel so cold
Who is Catherine?
Well, I don't know

What do I do?
Who is screaming?
Should I do that too?
I must be dreaming

What is that?
I can see a light
Wow, she must be fat
I'd better hold on tight

Why is it so bright?
My eyes are sore
I thought it was night
Oh, I feel so poor

Who is she?
Why is she tall?
I really want my tea
And a cuddle, that's all

Where am I?
Who are you?
What am I doing here?
What shall I do?

Nicola Weaver (11)
Tividale Community Arts College, Tividale

Love

Love is like a ball
It bounces back and back
But when your heart is broken
You shouldn't hear a crack.

Love is like a flower
The petals grow and grow
But when you've found the right boy
The power seems to flow.

Love is like a cake
It's not too hard to make
But when the cake doesn't rise quite right
Your heart will start to flake.

Love is like a pattern
It's pretty while it's there
But if you want to push me back
My heart will slightly tear.

Rhianna Centurion-Eyre (11)
Tudor Grange School, Solihull

The Day When Nobody Dies

Realising how small we are as I
Am staring up at the stars at night
Noticing the way we have become
The way we quarrel and how we fight.

Killing the life that keeps us alive while
Silencing secrets yet to be told
Judging others on ignorant views and
Leaving children dying, hungry and cold.

Firing bullets powered by greed and sin
The meaning of peace is no longer known
Persistently polluting our breath, our lives
Ignoring the tears of the depressed and alone.

Just imagine what the world could be
If everyone loved and swallowed their pride
If we share, thought of others before ourselves
Then the day would come when nobody dies.

Amelia Ebdon (15)
Tudor Grange School, Solihull

Trade

Crack! Crack!
The slithering slap of the white man's whip,
A venomous snake that's been uncoiled.
The ravenous wind consumes their breath,
As they struggle through their tattering toils.

Whoosh! Whoosh!
The swivelling splash of the ocean's turn,
Its green-tinged eyes turn towards a ship.
It is filled with ghostly citizens,
Who are held so tight by its firm, firm grip.

Sing! Sing!
The fine-tuned notes of the church's organ,
Accompanied by the saintly choir.
While through the glass still slaves are chained,
The singers sing to their Messiah.

Chime! Chime!
The conundrum cry from the ancient clock,
As it calls throughout the desperate quay.
But as the dirty deals are done,
No one stops to hear its plea.

So as the splatter of the pattering rain,
Obscures their hope from sight,
The slaves are left to wander on,
Like shadows in the night.

David Todd (15)
Tudor Grange School, Solihull

The Foggy Meadows

Away, away in the foggy meadows
Where sight is almost nil
The life around us is nearly dead
And everything is still

Carry on down the stream
Where water is full of grace
Oh, the stream 'tis like a dream
On a beautiful maiden's face

The trees sway from side to side
In a distance far ahead
The sight was such an everlasting joy
No words need be said

The chorus of the singing birds
Echoed in the air
Away, away from the foggy meadows
As if no one had been there.

James Henrick (11)
Tudor Grange School, Solihull

I Thought I Saw A Ballerina

I thought I saw a ballerina, dancing in the breeze
The shadow moved so swiftly, softly, I could not believe my eyes
The arms so soft, the body so textured, what was I to see?
So still and silent, yet gentle and smooth
Silently the ballerina moved with the wind as if it were music
Fulfilling its dream, dancing all day while other shadows stood still
and watched.
As I approached the gentle ballerina I wondered who it was
I never expected the silent, smooth ballerina to be a tall grown tree.

Felicity Zakers (12)
Tudor Grange School, Solihull

Guess

Millions of identical shooting stars,
Hands reaching out to catch them,
A vision of green,
Red, orange or brown,
A giant transformed from a stem.

A construction site within a life,
A magnificent natural tower,
Thousands of miniature blessings of Earth,
Feed upon its power.

Surbhi Kenth (14) & Emma Quirk (15)
Tudor Grange School, Solihull

Belief

My soul is covered in this bitter darkness,
Darkness. The twisted tale of another teen calamity
A thousand heartbeats I share,
The world which is close to its funeral day
Yet so far from its grave.
Dear, sweet imperfection,
Rid us of the exhausted cloud
That hangs above our heads.
Lies, lies. The substitute for faultless truth
Yet we'll wear it like a jewel.
And wonder why situations lie in such chaos
Chaos and confusion, when every day's a blur.
Yet we're all to blame, still
We'll have no shame.
As long as we're OK,
We'll find someone else to blame.
Tell us, God, what we're to do,
When every day's the same?

Emily Dean (13)
Tudor Grange School, Solihull

Thirteen

Unlucky for some
Unlucky for me you mean
I lost my best friend
I lost my boyfriend
My mom is ill and
So is my dad

My mom is annoyed
Because I'm rude and
Loud

My dad is annoyed
It's not my fault he
Moved away

My best friend hates me
Apparently I can't be
Trusted

My boyfriend hates me
Apparently I'm a waste
Of space

They don't understand
I've been through a lot you see
As I stand here alone in the world
Only thirteen.

Sophia Harley (13)
Tudor Grange School, Solihull

Missing Madeleine

I loved her so much, up to the heavens above
She is the one I will always love
But now she's missing, she makes no sound
And she won't stop crying until she is found

One day we went to Portugal, it started off good
We had so much fun and did what families should
But now she's missing, she makes no sound
And she won't stop crying until she is found

She was left with two kids, younger than her
They both were three, yes they really were
But now she's missing, she makes no sound
And she won't stop crying until she is found

We went to the shops, we told her to stay here
We weren't going far, we were just staying near
But now she's missing, she makes no sound
And she won't stop crying until she is found.

When we got back, there wasn't any sound
And when we searched, she was nowhere to be found
But now she's missing, she makes no sound
And she won't stop crying until she is found

I knew I shouldn't have done what I did
Why did I have to be so stupid?
But now she's missing, she makes no sound
And she won't stop crying until she is found

Whoever you are, give her to me
I do not want to lose my baby
But now she's missing, she makes no sound
And she won't stop crying until she is found.

Hans Ramzan (12)
Tudor Grange School, Solihull

To Skate Or Not To Skate?

To slip, to slide,
To move, to glide.
So scared was I to skate on ice.
With a *boom* and a *bang*, as I fell with wet hands.

People sad, people sorry,
As they moved from side to side with worry.
Some move elegantly
And others trip and stumble.

Terrified to slip and slide,
Like a tiger in a tornado,
From side to side I moved and grooved,
So amazed was I, like a proud petal.

As happy as a bouncy ball,
Amazed was I, I could stand and glide.
Everyone made it look so easy, and so did I,
As I moved in and out as smooth as ice,
To slip, to slide,
To move, to glide.

Fiona Pearce (13)
Tudor Grange School, Solihull

Young Writers Information

We hope you have enjoyed reading this book - and that you will continue to enjoy it in the coming years.

If you like reading and writing poetry drop us a line, or give us a call, and we'll send you a free information pack.

Alternatively if you would like to order further copies of this book or any of our other titles, then please give us a call or log onto our website at
www.youngwriters.co.uk

Young Writers Information
Remus House
Coltsfoot Drive
Peterborough
PE2 9JX
(01733) 890066